The Art of Poetry volume 18

Edexcel poetry: Time and Place

With thanks to Matthew Curry for his introduction to metre and to Freya for her encouragement.

Published by Peripeteia Press Ltd.

First published February 2018

ISBN: 978-1-9997376-3-4

Peripeteia.webs.com

Contents

General Introduction to the The Art of Poetry series

The philosopher Nietzsche described his work as 'the greatest gift that [mankind] has ever been given'. The Elizabethan poet Edmund Spenser hoped his book *The Faerie Queene* would magically transform its readers into noblemen. In comparison, our aims for *The Art of Poetry* series are a little more modest. Fundamentally we aim to provide books that will be of maximum use to English students and to their teachers. In our experience, few students read essays on poetry, yet, whatever specification they are studying, they have to write them. That seems like a significant oversight. So, we've offering a range of models, written in a lively and accessible, but also critical style. Our essays are not designed to be comprehensive, or to provide the one 'correct', authoritative reading of any of the set poems. Nor do we necessarily follow the same reading strategy in every essay. Instead we've focused on what we've found most interesting in each poem and developed our essays from that rather singular starting point. Inevitably the essays include a lot of fine-grained close analysis of language, form and structure, and we refer to contexts when we think they illuminate the text. But, overall, our essays are not designed to substitute for your own engagement with the poems or act as textual crutches. Rather they are intended to be springboards or launchpads for your own thinking. No doubts we will have missed things that you will find in the poems. And these things are all the more valuable if you discover them for yourself.

We believe too that the essay as a form needs championing, especially when so many revision books for students present information in broken down and simplified note form. If there's value in writing essays, there's a value in reading them too, surely. In this current volume, we turn our focus to GCSE, providing critical support for students reading poems about time and place from Edexcel's poetry anthology. In particular, we hope to inspire those students aiming to reach the very highest grades and those teachers who wish to make their poetry lessons as dynamic and engaging as possible.

4

Introduction to Volume 18: Time and Place

An adventure into what one apprehends

When writing about themes, students often simply state what they think the major theme of a poem to be. As Edexcel has kindly arranged these poems as a thematic cluster, writing something like 'this is a poem about places' doesn't get you very far. Sometimes readers also labour under misconceptions about the nature of poetry, believing, for example, that poems have secret meanings that, rather annoyingly, poets have hidden under deliberately obscure language. The task of the reader becomes to decode the obscure language and extract the hidden message. Unsurprisingly, this misconception of poetry as a sort of self-regarding subcategory of fables makes readers wonder why poets go to all the irritating trouble of hiding their messages in the first place. If they had something to say, why didn't the poet just say it and save everyone a lot of unnecessary fuss and bother? Why couldn't Blake, for instance, have just said that London was a corrupt and corrupting city?

The Romantic poet, John Keats's comment about distrusting poetry that has a 'palpable design' on the reader has been much quoted. For Keats, and many poets, a 'palpable design' is an aspect of rhetoric and particularly of propaganda and a poem is not just a piece of propaganda for a poet's ideas. As the modern poet, George Szirtes puts it, poems are not 'rhymed advertisements for the already formed views of poets'. Here's George discussing the issue in his blog [ttp://georgeszirtes.blogspot.co.uk/]: 'A proper poem has to be a surprise: no surprise for the poet no surprise for the reader, said Robert Frost and I think that he and Keats were essentially right. A proper poem should arise out of a naked unguarded experience that elicits surprise in the imagination by extending the consciousness in some way. Poetry is not what one knows but an adventure into what one apprehends.'

Most poems are not merely prettified presentations of a poet's settled views about a particular theme or issue; they are more like thought experiments or journeys of exploration and discovery. In other words, poetry, like all art, is equipment for thinking and feeling. So, instead of writing that 'poem x is about time and place' try to think more carefully through what is interesting or unusual or surprising about the poem's exploration of these subjects. Sometimes the role of the time and place in a poem might be obvious, as in poems such as *Nothing's Changed*. At other times the place might be a backdrop to a poem focused more on character, as in Hannah's poem. Approach a poem with questions in mind: What does the poem have to say about its theme? What angle does the poet take; is the poem celebratory, mournful, exploratory? To what extent does the poem take up arms and argue for something and have a 'palpable design'? Is the attitude to the subject consistent or does it change? To what extent is the poem philosophical or emotional? Do we learn something new, does it change how we think or feel? How might the poem have extended our thinking about its subject?

Clearly some of these poems explore how where we live and grow up affects our sense of identity. To what extent do you think of yourself as a citizen of the world or as European? Or do you think of yourself as predominantly British or Welsh, Scottish, English or Indian English or Caribbean English? Or do you identify more with being a region – a Southerner, Northerner or Midlander – with a city – Londoner, Brummie – or with the countryside? How do you feel about your local environ, the city or suburb or town or village? Are you proud of where you live? If they are different places, do you align yourself with where you were born or with where you live now? Or is your sense of self more determined by your age and when you were born? Are you part of a distinct generation? Some sociologists argue that people born within particular decades tend to share similar attitudes and values? To what extent do you think your values and attitudes have been shaped by when you were born?

Not all of the poems in this collection are, however, about place and identity. In other poems places are significant because they are tied to incidents, memories and to specific people. In others, the aesthetics of a time or place is key to determining the poet's feelings. These poems span a few hundred years and stretch from America to South Africa, from New Zealand to Pakistan, and from the Caribbean to England and Italy. One poem is even set in the sky. The poems feature urban landscapes, parks and gardens, the coast and the sea and the English countryside. Together they provide a compelling meditation of the power of places and times in shaping who we are and how we live.

An adventure into what you apprehend is a great way to conceptualise a poem. And it's very productive too as a way to think about writing poetry criticism, to which theme we turn next.

How to analyse a poem [seen and unseen]

A list of ingredients, not a recipe

Firstly, what not to do: sometimes pupils have been so programmed to spot poetic features such as alliteration that they start analysis of a poem with close reading of these micro aspects of technique in isolation. This is never a good idea. A far better strategy is to begin by trying to develop an overall understanding of what the poem is about. While, obviously, all these poems are about time and place, the nature of the of settings vary widely and what the poets have say about this theme is also highly varied. Once you've established the central concerns, you can delve into the poem's interior, examining its inner workings in the light of these. And you should be flexible enough to adapt, refine or even reject your initial thoughts in the light of your investigation. The essential point is to make sure that whether you're discussing imagery or stanza form, sonic effects or syntax, enjambment or vocabulary, you always explore the significance of the feature in terms of meanings and effects.

Someone once compared texts to cakes. When you're presented with a cake the first thing you notice is what it looks like. Probably the next thing you'll do is taste it and find out if you like the flavour. This aesthetic experience will come first. Only later might you investigate the ingredients and how it was made. Adopting a uniform reading strategy is like a recipe; it sets out what you must, do step by step, in a predetermined order. This can be helpful, especially when you start reading and analysing poems. Hence in our first volume in *The Art of Poetry* series we explored each poem under the same subheadings of narrator, characters, imagery, patterns of sound, form & structure and contexts, and all our essays followed essentially the same general direction. Of course, this is a reasonable strategy for reading poetry and will stand you in good stead. However, this present volume takes a different, more flexible approach, because this book is designed for students aiming for levels 7 to 9, or A to A* in old currency, and to reach the highest levels your work needs to be a bit more conceptual, critical and individual. Writing frames are useful for beginners, like stabilisers when you learn to ride a bike. But, if you wish to write top level essays you need to develop your own frames.

Read our essays and you'll find that they all include the same principle ingredients – detailed, 'fine-grained' reading of crucial elements of poetry, imagery, form, rhyme and so forth - but each essay starts in a different way and each one has a slightly different focus or weight of attention on the various aspects that make up a poem. Once you feel you have mastered the apprentice strategy of reading all poems in the same way, we strongly recommend you put any generic essay recipe approach you've been given to one side and move on to a new way of reading, an approach flexible enough to change depending on the nature of the poem you're reading.

Follow your nose

Having established what you think a poem is about - its theme and what is interesting about the poet's treatment of the theme [the conceptual bit], rather than then working through a pre-set agenda, decide what you honestly think are the most interesting aspects of the poem and start analysing these closely. This way your response will be distinctive, and you'll quickly be writing about material you find most interesting. In other words, you're foregrounding yourself as an individual, critical reader. These most interesting aspects might be ideas or technique based, or both.

So, follow your own, informed instincts, trust in your critical intelligence as a reader. If you're writing about material that genuinely interests you, your writing is likely to be interesting for the examiner too. And, obviously, take advice from your teacher too, use their expertise. Keep an eye too on the nature of the question you're answering.

Because of the focus on sonic effects and imagery other aspects of poems are often overlooked by students. It is a rare student, for instance, who notices how punctuation works in a poem and who can write about it convincingly. Few students write about the contribution of the unshowy function words, such as pronouns, prepositions or conjunctions, yet these words are crucial to any text. Of course, it would be a highly risky strategy to focus your whole essay on a seemingly innocuous and incidental detail of a poem. But noticing what others do not, and coming at things from an unusual angle are as important to writing great essays as they are to the production of great poetry.

So, in summary, when reading a poem have a check list in mind, but don't feel you must follow someone else's generic essay recipe. Don't feel that you must always start with a consideration of imagery if the poem you're analysing has, for instance, an eye-catching form. Consider the significance of major features, such as imagery, vocabulary, sonic patterns and form. Try to write about these aspects in terms of their contribution to themes and effects. Try to see too how these various aspects work in relation to each other. Follow your nose, find your own direction, seek out aspects that genuinely engage you and write about these. Try to develop your own essay style.

The essays in this volume provide examples and we hope they will encourage you to go your own way, at least to some extent, and to make discoveries for yourself. No single essay could possibly cover everything that could be said about any one of these poems; aiming to create comprehensive essays like this would be utterly foolish and would require a much longer, perhaps even endless book. And hence we have not tried to do so. Nor are our essays meant to be models for exam essays – they're far too long for that. They do, however, illustrate the sort of conceptualised, critical and 'fine-grained' exploration demanded for top grades at GCSE and beyond. As we've said, there's always more to be discovered, more to say, space in other words for you to develop some original reading of your own, space for you to write your own individual essay recipe.

Writing literature essays

The BIG picture and the small

An essay itself can be a form of art. And writing a great essay takes time, skill and practice. And also expert advice. Study the two figures in the picture carefully and describe what you can see. Channel your inner Sherlock Holmes to add any deductions you are able to form about the image. Before reading what we have to say, write your description out as a prose paragraph. Probably you'll have written something along the following lines:

First off, the overall impression: this picture is very blurry. Probably this indicates that either this is a very poor-quality reproduction, or that it is a copy of a very small detail from a much bigger image that has been magnified several times. The image shows a stocky man and a medium-sized dog, both orientated towards something to their left, which suggests there is some point of interest in that direction. From the man's rustic dress (smock, breeches, clog-like boots) the picture is either an old one or a modern one depicting the past. The man appears to be carrying a stick and there's maybe a bag on his back. From all of these details we can probably deduce that he's a peasant, maybe a farmer or a shepherd.

Now do the same thing for picture two. We have even less detail here and again the picture's blurry. Particularly without the benefit of colour, it's hard to determine what we're, seeing other than a horizon and maybe the sky. We might just be able to make out that in the centre of the picture is the shape of the sun. From the reflection, we can deduce that the image is of the sun either setting or rising over water. If it is dawn this usually symbolises hope, birth and new beginnings; if the sun is setting it conventionally symbolises the opposite – the end of things, the coming of night/ darkness, death.

If you're a sophisticated reader, you might well start to think about links between the two images. Are they, perhaps, both details from the same single larger image, for instance.

Well, this image might be even harder to work out. Now we don't even have a  whole figure, just a leg, is it [?], sticking up in the air. Whatever is happening here, it looks painful and we can't even see the top half of the body. From the upside orientation, we might guess that the figure is or has fallen. If we put this image with the one above, we might think the figure has fallen into water as there are horizontal marks on the image that could be splashes. From the quality of this image we can deduce that this is an even smaller detail blown-up.

You may be wondering by now why we've suddenly moved into rudimentary art appreciation. On the other hand, you may already have worked out the point of this exercise. Either way, bear with us, because this is the last picture for you to describe and analyse. So, what have we here?  Looks like another peasant, again from the past, perhaps medieval (?) from the smock-like dress, clog-like shoes and the britches. This character is also probably male and seems to be pushing some wooden apparatus from left to right. From the ridges at the bottom left of the image we can surmise that he's working the land, probably driving a plough. Noticeably the figure has his back to us; we see his turned away from us, suggesting his whole concentration is on the task at hand. In the background appear to be sheep, which would fit with our impression that this is an image of farming. It seems likely that this image and the first one come from the same painting. They have a similar style and subject and it is possible that these sheep belong to our first character. This image is far less blurry than the other one. Either it is a better-quality reproduction, or this is a larger, more significant detail extracted from the original source. If this is a significant detail it's interesting that we cannot see the character's face. From this we can deduce that he's not important in and of himself; rather he's a representative figure and the important thing is what he is and what he isn't looking at.

Okay, we hope we haven't stretched your patience too far. What's the point of all this? Well, let's imagine we prefixed the paragraphs above with an introduction, along the following lines: 'The painter makes this picture interesting and powerful by using several key techniques and details' and that we added a conclusion, along the lines of 'So now I have shown how the painter has made this picture interesting and powerful through the use of several key techniques and details'. Finally, substitute painter and picture for writer and text. If we put together our paragraphs into an essay what would be its strengths and weaknesses? What might be a better way of writing our essay?

Consider the strengths first off. The best bits of our essay, we humbly suggest, are the bits where we begin to explain what we are seeing, when we do the Holmes like deductive thinking. Another strength might be that we have started to make links between the various images, or parts of a larger image, to see how they work together to provide us more information. A corresponding weakness is that each of our paragraphs seems like a separate chunk of writing. The weaker parts of the paragraphs are where we simply describe what we can see. More importantly though, if we used our comments on image one as our first paragraph we seem to have started in a rather random way. Why should we have begun our essay with that image? What was the logic behind that? And most importantly of all, if this image is an analogue for a specific aspect of a text, such as a poem's imagery or a novel's dialogue we have dived straight into to analysing this technical aspect before we're established any overall sense of the painting/ text. And this is a very common fault with GCSE English Literature essays. As we've said before and will keep saying, pupils start writing detailed micro-analysis of a detail such as alliteration before they have established the big picture of what the text is about and what the answer to the question they've been set might be. Without this big picture it's very difficult to write about the significance of the micro details. And the major marks for English essays are reserved for explanations of the significance and effects generated by a writer's craft.

Now we'll try a different and much better approach. Let's start off with the big picture, the whole image. The painting above is *Landscape with the fall of Icarus*. It's usually attributed to the Renaissance artist, Pieter Breughel and was probably painted in the 1560s. Icarus is a character from Greek mythology. He was the son of the brilliant inventor, Daedalus. Trapped on Crete by the evil King Minos, Daedalus and Icarus managed to escape when the inventor created pairs of giant feathered wings. Before they took to sky Daedalus warned his son not to get too excited and fly too near the sun as the wings were held together by wax that might melt. Icarus didn't listen, however. The eventual result was that he plummeted back to earth, into the sea more precisely and was killed.

Applying this contextual knowledge to the painting we can see that the image is about how marginal Icarus' tragedy is in the big picture. Conventionally we'd expect any image depicting such a famous myth to make Icarus's fall the dramatic centre of attention. The main objects of this painting, however, are emphatically not the falling boy hitting the water. Instead our eye is drawn to the peasant in the centre of the painting, pushing his plough (even more so in colour as his shirt is the only red object in an otherwise greeny-yellow landscape) and the stately galleon sailing calmly past those protruding legs. Seeing the whole image, we can appreciate the significance of the shepherd and the ploughman looking up and down and to the left. The point being made is how they don't even notice the tragedy because they have work to do and need to get on with their lives. The animals too seem unconcerned. As W. H. Auden puts it, in lines from *Musée des Beaux Arts*, 'everything turns away / Quite leisurely from the disaster'.

To sum up, when writing an essay on any literary text do not begin with close-up analysis of micro-details. Begin instead with establishing the whole picture: What the text is about, what key techniques the writer uses, when it was written, what sort of text it is, what effects it has on the reader. Then, when you zoom in to examine smaller details, such as imagery, individual words, metre or sonic techniques you can discuss these in relation to their significance in terms of this bigger picture.

What would our art appreciation essay look like now?

Paragraph #1: Introduction – myth of Icarus, date of painting, the way our eyes is drawn away from his tragic death to much more ordinary life going around him. Significance of this – even tragic suffering goes on around us without us even noticing, we're too busy getting on with our lives.

Paragraph #2: We could, of course, start with our first figure and follow the same order as we've presented the images here. But wouldn't it make more logical sense to discuss first the biggest, more prominent images in the painting first? So, our first paragraph is about the ploughman and his horse. How his figure placed centrally and is bent downwards towards the ground and turned left away from us etc.

Paragraph #3: The next most prominent image is the ship. Also moving from right to left, as if the main point of interest in the painting is off in that direction. Here we could consider the other human agricultural figure, the shepherd and his dog and, of course, the equally oblivious sheep.

Paragraph #4: Having moved on to examining background details in the painting we could discuss the symbolism of the sun on the horizon. While this could be the sun rising, the context of the story suggests it is more likely to be setting. The pun of the sun/son going down makes sense.

Paragraph #5: Finally, we can turn our attention to the major historical and literary figure in this painting, Icarus and how he is presented. This is the key image in terms of understanding the painting's purpose and effect.

Paragraph #6: Conclusion. What is surprising about this picture. How do the choices the painter makes affect us as viewer/ reader? Does this painting make Icarus's story seem more pathetic, more tragic or something else?

Now, all you have to do is switch from a painting to a poem.

Big pictures, big cakes, recipes and lists of instructions; following your own nose and going your own way. Whatever metaphors we use, your task is to bring something personal and individual to your critical reading of poems and to your essay writing.

Writing comparative essays

The following is adapted from our discussion of this topic in *The Art of Writing English Literature Essay*s A-level course companion, and is a briefer version, tailored to the GCSE exam task. Fundamentally, comparative essays want you to display not only your ability to intelligently talk about literary texts, but also your ability to make meaningful connections between them. The first starting point is your topic. This must be broad enough to allow substantial thematic overlapping of the texts. However, too little overlap and it will be difficult to connect the texts; too much overlap and your discussion will be lopsided and one-dimensional. In the case of the GCSE exam, the broad topic will, of course, be relationships. The exam question will ask you to focus on the methods used by the poets to explore how two poems present this theme. You will also be directed to write specifically on language and imagery [AO2] as well as on the contexts in which the poems were written [AO3].

One poem from the anthology will be specified and printed on the paper. You will then have to choose a companion poem. Selecting the right poem for interesting comparison is obviously very important. Obviously, you should prepare for this task beforehand by pairing up the poems, especially as you will only have about 35 minutes to complete this task. You will also be asked to compare unseen poems, so grasping how best to write comparative essays is essential to your chance of reaching the top grades. To think about this task visually, you don't want Option A, below, [not enough overlap] or Option B [two much overlap]. You want Option C. This option allows substantial common links to be built between your chosen texts where discussion arises from both fundamental similarities AND differences.

Option A: too many differences

Option B: too many similarities

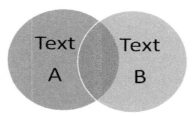

Option C: suitable number of similarities and differences

The final option will generate the most interesting discussion as it will allow substantial similarities to emerge as well as differences. <u>The best comparative essays actually find that what seemed like clear similarities become subtle differences and vice versa</u> while still managing to find rock solid similarities to build their foundations on.

Check the mark scheme for this question and you'll notice that to reach the top grade your comparison must be 'well-structured'. How should you structure a comparative essay? Consider the following alternatives. Which one is best and why?

Essay Structure #1
1. Introduction
2. Main body paragraph #1 - Text A
3. Main body paragraph #2 - Text A
4. Main body paragraph #3 - Text B
5. Main body paragraph #4 - Text B
6. Conclusion

Essay Structure #2
1. Introduction
2. Main body paragraph #1 - Text A
3. Main body paragraph #2 - Text A
4. Main body paragraph #3 - Text B
5. Main body paragraph #4 - Text B
6. Comparison of main body paragraphs #1 & #3 - Text A + B
7. Comparison of main body paragraphs #2 & #4 - Text A + B
8. Conclusion

Essay Structure #3
1. Introduction
2. Main body paragraph #1 - Text A + B
3. Main body paragraph #2 - Text A + B
4. Main body paragraph #3 - Text A + B
5. Main body paragraph #4 - Text A + B
6. Conclusion

We hope you will agree that 3 is the optimum option. Option 1 is the dreaded 'here is everything I know about text A, followed by everything I know by Text B' approach where the examiner has to work out what the connections are between the texts. This will score the lowest marks. Option 2 is better: There is some attempt to compare the two texts. However, it is a very inefficient way of comparing the two texts. For comparative essay writing the most important thing is to discuss both texts together. This is the most effective and efficient way of achieving your overall aim. Option 3 does this by comparing and contrasting the two texts under common umbrella headings. This naturally encourages comparison. Using comparative discourse markers, such as 'similarly', 'in contrast to', 'conversely' 'likewise' and 'however' also facilitates effective comparison.

When writing about each poem, make sure you do not work chronologically through a poem, summarising the content of each stanza. Responses of this sort typically start with 'In the first stanza' and employ discourse markers of time rather than comparison, such as 'after', 'next', 'then' and so forth. Even if your reading is analytical rather than summative, your essay should not work through the poem from the opening to the ending. Instead, make sure you write about the ideas explored in both texts [themes], the feelings and effects generated and the techniques the poets utilise to achieve these.

Writing about language

Poems are paintings as well as windows; we look at them as well as through them. As you know, special attention should be paid to language in poetry because of all the literary art forms poetry, in particular, employs language in a precise, self-conscious and distinctive way. Ideally in poetry, every word should count. Analysis of language falls into distinct categories:

- By diction we mean the vocabulary used in a poem. A poem might be composed from the ordinary language of everyday speech or it might use elaborate, technical or elevated phrasing. Or both. At one time, some words and types of words were considered inappropriate for the rarefied field of poetry. The great Irish poet, W. B. Yeats never referred to modern technology in his poetry, there are no cars, or tractors or telephones, because he did not consider such things fitting for poetry. When much later, Philip Larkin used swear words in his otherwise well-mannered verse the effect was deeply shocking. Modern poets have pretty much dispensed with the idea of there being an elevated literary language appropriate for poetry. Hence in the Edexcel anthology you'll find all sorts of modern, everyday language.

- Grammatically a poem may use complex or simple sentences [the key to which is the conjunctions]; it might employ a wash of adjectives and adverbs, or it may rely extensively on the bare force of nouns and verbs. Picking out and exploring words from specific grammatical classes has the merit of being both incisive and usually illuminating.

- Poets might mix together different types, conventions and registers of language, moving, for example, between formal and informal, spoken and written, modern and archaic, and so forth. Arranging the diction in the poem in terms of lexico-semantic fields, by register or by etymology, helps reveal underlying patterns of meaning.

- For almost all poems imagery is a crucial aspect of language. Broadly imagery is a synonym for description and can be broken down into two types, sensory and figurative. Sensory imagery means the words and phrases that appeal to our senses, to touch and taste, hearing, smell and sight. Sensory imagery is evocative; it helps to take us into the world of the poem to share the experience being described. Figurative imagery, in particular, is always significant. As we have mentioned, not all poems rely on metaphors and similes; these devices are only part of a poet's box of tricks, but figurative language is always important when it occurs because it compresses multiple meanings into itself. To use a technical term figurative images are polysemic - they contain many meanings. Try writing out the all the meanings contained in a metaphor in a more concise and economical way. Even simple, everyday metaphors compress meaning. If we want to say our teacher is fierce and powerful and that we fear his or her wrath, we can more concisely say our teacher is a dragon.

Writing about patterns of sound

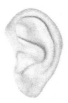 Like painters, some poets have powerful visual imaginations, while other poets have stronger auditory imaginations and are more like musicians. And some poems are like paintings, others are more like pieces of music.

Firstly, what not to do: Tempting as it may be to spot sonic features of a poem and list these, don't do this. Avoid something along the lines of 'The poet uses alliteration here and the rhyme scheme is ABABCDCDEFEFGG'. Sometimes, indeed, it may be tempting to set out the poem's whole rhyme scheme like this. Resist the temptation: This sort of identification of features is worth zero marks. Marks in exams are reserved for attempts to link techniques to meanings and to effects.

Probably many of us have been sitting in English lessons listening somewhat sceptically as our English teacher explains the surprisingly specific significance of a seemingly random piece of alliteration in a poem. Something along the lines 'The double d sounds here reinforce a sense of invincible strength' or 'the harsh repetition of the 't' sounds suggests anger'. Through all our minds at some point may have passed the idea that, in these instances, English teachers appear to be using some sort of Enigma-style secret symbolic decoding machine that reveals how particular patterns of sounds have such definite encoded meanings.

And this sort of thing is not all nonsense. Originally deriving from an oral tradition, poems are, of course, written for the ear as much as for the eye, to be heard as much as read. A poem is a soundscape as much as it is a set of meanings. Sounds are, however, difficult to tie to very definite meanings and effects. By way of example, the old BBC Radiophonic workshop, which produced ambient sounds for radio and television programmes, used the same sounds in different contexts, knowing that the audience would perceive them in the appropriate way because of that context. Hence the sound of bacon sizzling, of an audience clapping and of feet walking over gravel were actually recordings of an identical sound. Listeners heard them differently because of the context. So, we may, indeed, be able to spot the repeated 's' sounds in a poem, but whether this creates a hissing sound, yes like a snake, or the susurration of the sea will depend on the context within the poem and the ears of the reader. Whether a sound is soft and soothing or harsh and grating is also open to interpretation.

The idea of connecting these sounds to meanings or significance is a productive one. And your analysis will be most convincing if you use several pieces of evidence together. In other words, rather than try to pick out individual examples of sonic effects we recommend you explore the weave or pattern of sounds, the effects these generate and their contribution to feelings and ideas. For example, this might mean examining how alliteration and assonance are used together to achieve a particular mimetic effect.

Writing about form & structure

As you know, there are no marks for simply identifying textual features. This holds true for language, sounds and also for form. Consider instead the relationship between a poem's form and its content, themes and effects. Form is not merely decorative or ornamental: A poem's meanings and effects are generated through the interplay of form and content. Broadly speaking the form can either work with or against a poem's content. Conventionally a sonnet, for instance, is about love, whereas a limerick is a comic form. A serious love poem in the form of a limerick would be unusual, as would a sonnet about an old man with a beard.

Sometimes poetic form can create an ironic backdrop to highlight an aspect of content. An example would be a formally elegant poem about something or

somewhere monstrous. Blake's *London* might spring to mind. The artist Grayson Perry uses form in this ironic way. Rather than depicting the sort of picturesque, idealised images we expect of ceramics, Perry's pots and urns depict modern life in bright, garish colours. The urn pictured, for instance, is entitled *Modern Family* and depicts two gay men with a boy who they have presumably adopted. A thrash metal concert inside a church, a philosophical essay via text message, a fine crystal goblet filled with cherryade

would be further examples of ironic relationships or tension between message and medium, content and context or form. *In How to Read Literature*, Terry Eagleton gives similar examples, such as a monumental poem about a mouse and a poem expressing a 'yearning to be free in a strict, straitjacketing kind of metre'.[1]

****

How to Read Literature, p.3.

Reading form

Put a poem before your eyes. Start off taking a panoramic perspective: Think of the forest, not the trees. Perhaps mist over your eyes a bit. Don't even read the words, just look at the poem, like at a painting. Is the poem slight, thin, fat, long, short? What is the relation of whiteness to blackness? Why might the poet have chosen this shape? Does it look regular or irregular? A poem about a long winding river will probably look rather different from one about a small pebble, or really should do. Unless form is being employed ironically. Now read the poem a couple of times. First time, fast as you can, second time more slowly and carefully. How does the visual layout of the poem relate to what it seems to be about? Does this form support, or create a tension against, the content? Is the form one you recognise, like a sonnet, or is it more open, more irregular like free verse? Usually the latter is obvious from the irregularity of the stanzas, line lengths and lack of metre or rhyme.

As Hurley and O'Neill explain in *Poetic Form: An Introduction*, like genre, form sets expectations: 'In choosing form, poets bring into play associations and expectations which they may then satisfy, modify or subvert'. We've already suggested that if we see a poem is a sonnet or a limerick this recognition will set up expectations about the nature of the poem's content. The same thing works on a smaller level; once we have noticed that a poem's first stanza is a quatrain, we expect it to continue in this neat, orderly fashion. If the quatrain's rhyme scheme is xaxa, xbxb, in which only the second and fourth lines rhyme, we reasonably expect that the next stanza will be xcxc. So, if it isn't we need to consider why.

After taking in the big picture in terms of choice of form in relation to content zoom in: Explore the stanza form, lineation, punctuation, the use of enjambment and caesura. Single line stanzas draw attention to themselves. If they are end-stopped they can suggest isolation, separation. Couplets imply twoness. Stanzas of three lines are called tercets and feature in villanelles and terza rima. On the page, both these forms tend to look rather delicate, especially if separated from each other by the silence of white space. Often balanced through rhyme, quatrains look a bit more robust and sturdy. Cinquains are swollen quatrains in which the last line often seems to throw the stanza out of balance.

Focus in on specific examples and on points of transition. For instance, if a poem has four regular quatrains followed by a couplet, examine the effect of this change. If we've been ticking along nicely in iambic metre and suddenly trip on a trochee, examine why. Consider regularity. Closed forms of poems, such as sonnets, are highly regular with set rhyme schemes, metre and number of lines. The opposite form is called 'open', the most extreme version of which is free verse. In free verse poems, the poet dispenses with any set metre, rhyme scheme or recognisable traditional form. What stops this sort of poetry from being prose chopped up to look like verse? The care of the design on the page. Hence, we need to focus here on lineation. Enjambment runs over lines and makes connections; caesura pauses a line and separates words. Lots of enjambment generates a sense of the language running away from the speaker. Lots of caesuras generate a halting, hesitant, choppy movement to lines. Opposites, these devices work in tandem and where they fall is always significant in a good poem.

Remember poetic form is never merely decorative. And bear in mind too the fact that the most volatile materials require the strongest containers.

Nice to metre...

A brief guide to metre and rhythm in poetry

Why express yourself in poetry? Why read words dressed up and expressed as a poem? What can you get from poetry that you can't from prose? There are many compelling answers to these questions. Here, though, we're going to concentrate on one aspect of the unique appeal of poetry – the structure of sound in poetry. Whatever our stage of education, we are all already sophisticated at detecting and using structured sound. Try reading the following sentences without any variation whatsoever in how each sound is emphasised,  and they will quickly lose what essential human characteristics they have. The sentences will sound robotic. So, in a sense, we won't be teaching anything new here. It's just that in poetry the structure of sound is carefully unusually crafted and created. It becomes a key part of what a poem is.

We will introduce a few new key technical terms along the way, but the ideas are straightforward. Individual sounds [syllables] are either stressed [emphasised, sounding louder and longer] or unstressed. As well as clustering into words and sentences for meaning, these sounds [syllables] cluster into rhythmic groups or feet, producing the poem's metre, which is the characteristic way its rhythm works.

In some poems, the rhythm is very regular and may even have a name, such as iambic pentameter. At the other extreme a poem may have no discernible regularity at all. As we have said, this is called free verse. It is vital to remember that the sound in a good poem is structured so that it combines effectively with the meanings.

For example, take a look at these two lines from Marvell's *To his Coy Mistress*:
'But at my back I alwaies hear
Times winged Chariot hurrying near:'

Forgetting the rhythms for a moment, Marvell is basically saying at this point 'Life is short, Time flies, and it's after us'. Now concentrate on the rhythm of his words.

- In the first line every other syllable is stressed: 'at', 'back', 'al', 'hear'.
- Each syllable before these is unstressed 'But', 'my', 'I', 'aies'.
- This is a regular beat or rhythm which we could write
  ti TUM / ti TUM / ti TUM / ti TUM , with the / separating the feet. ['Feet' is the technical term for metrical units of sound]
- This type of two beat metrical pattern is called iambic, and because there are four feet in the line, it is tetrameter. So this line is in 'iambic tetrameter'. [Tetra is Greek for four]
- Notice that 'my' and 'I' being unstressed diminishes the speaker, and we are already prepared for what is at his 'back', what he can 'hear' to be bigger than him, since these sounds are stressed.
- On the next line, the iambic rhythm is immediately broken off, since the next line hits us with two consecutive stressed syllables straight off: 'Times' 'wing'. Because a pattern had been established, when it suddenly changes the reader feels it, the words feel crammed together more urgently, the beats of the rhythm are closer, some little parcels of time have gone missing.

A physical rhythmic sensation is created of time slipping away, running out. This subtle sensation is enhanced by the stress-unstress-unstress pattern of words that follow, 'chariot hurrying' [TUM-ti-ti, TUM-ti-ti]. So the hurrying sounds underscore the meaning of the words.

14 ways of looking at a poem

Though conceived as pre-reading exercises, most of these tasks work just as well for revision.

1. Mash them (1) – mix together lines from two or more poems. The students' task is to untangle the poems from each other.

2. Mash them (2) – the second time round make the task significantly harder. Rather than just mixing whole lines, mash the poems together more thoroughly, words, phrases, images and all, so that unmashing seems impossible. At first sight.

3. Dock the last stanza or few lines from a poem. The students should come up with their own endings for the poem. Compare with the poet's version. Or present the poem without its title. Can the students come up with a suitable one?

4. Break a poem into segments. Split the class into groups. Each group work in isolation on their segment and feedback on what they discover. Then their task is to fit the poem and their ideas about it together as a whole.

5. Give the class the first and last stanza of a poem. Their task is to provide the filling. They can choose to attempt the task at beginner level (in prose) or at world class level (in poetry).

6. Add superfluous words to a poem. Start off with obvious interventions, such as the interjection of blatantly alien, noticeable words. Try smuggling 'pineapple', 'bourbon' and 'haberdashers' into any of the poems and see if you can get it past the critical sensors.

7. Repeat the exercise – This time using much less extravagant words. Try to smuggle in a few intensifiers, such as 'really', 'very' and 'so'. Or extra adjectives.

8. Collapse the lineation in a poem and present it as continuous prose. The students' task is to put it back into verse. Discussing the various pros and cons or various possible arrangements – short lines, long lines, irregular lines - can be very productive. Pay particular attention to line breaks and the words that end them. After a whatever-time-you- deem-fit, give the class the pattern of the first stanza. They then have to decide how to arrange the next stanza. Drip feed the rest of the poem to them.

9. Find a way to present the shapes of each poem on the page without the words. The class should work through each poem, two minutes at a time, speculating on what the shape might tell us about the content of the poem. This exercise works especially well as a starter activity. We recommend you use two poems at a time, as the comparison helps students to recognise and appreciate different shapes.

10. Test the thesis that an astute reader can recognise poems by men from those written by women. Give the class one of the poems such as *London* or *I Started Early* without the name of the poet. Ask them to identify whether the writer is male or female and to explain their reasons for identifying them as such.

11. Split the class into groups. Each group should focus their analysis on a different feature of the poem. Start with the less obvious aspects: Group 1 should concentrate on enjambment and caesuras; group 2 on punctuation; group 3 on the metre and rhythm; group 4 on function words – conjunctions, articles, prepositions. 2-5 mins. only. Then swap focus, four times. Share findings.

12. In *Observations on Poetry*, Robert Graves wrote that 'rhymes properly used are the good servants whose presence at the dinner-table gives

the guests a sense of opulent security; never awkward or over-clever, they hand the dishes silently and professionally. You can trust them not to interrupt the conversation or allow their personal disagreements to come to the notice of the guests; but some of them are getting very old for their work'. Explore the poets' use of rhyme in the light of Graves' comment. Are the rhymes ostentatiously original or old hat? Do they stick out of the poem or are they neatly tucked in? Are they dutiful servants of meaning or noisy disrupters of the peace?

13. The Romantic poet, John Keats, claimed that 'we hate poetry that has a palpable design upon us – and if we do not agree seems to put its hand its breeches pock'. Apply his comment to this selection of poems. Do any seem to have a 'palpable design' on the reader? If so, how does the poem want us to respond?

14. Each student should crunch the poem down to one word per line. Discuss this process as a class. Project the poem so the whole class can see it and start the crunching process by indicating and then crossing-out the function words from each line. Now discuss which of the remaining words is most important. This will also give you an opportunity to refer to grammatical terms, such as nouns and verbs. Once each line has been reduced to one word, from this list, pupils should crunch again. This time all that should remain are the five most important words in the whole poem. Now they need to write two or three sentences for each of these words explaining exactly why they are so important and why the poet didn't choose any of the possible synonyms.

'Poetry is only there to frame the silence. There is silence between each verse and silence at the end.'

ALICE OSWALD

John Keats, *To Autumn*

Load every rift with ore

In his fascinating poetry primer, *The Secret Life of Poems*, poet and critic Tom Paulin argues that *To Autumn* is a coded political allegory responding to contemporary events such as the Peterloo Massacre and government infringements of liberty. To my mind, Paulin's Marxist reading may be brilliant, but it is also a little tenuous, requiring some tendentious linguistic gymnastics to contort the poem to fit the interpretation. A couple of examples: Paulin argues Keats' use of the word 'sun' in the first line inevitably conjures a specific, loaded rhyme word. Think of a few possibilities for a moment and you might come up with 'run', 'fun', 'pun', 'stun', 'bun', 'spun', 'done'. But Paulin insists that readers automatically arrive at 'gun' which then evokes the violence of the Peterloo

Massacre. [If your first thought was also 'gun', perhaps this is because I try to trigger this with the adjective 'loaded', but there's no trigger in Keats' poem.] Similarly, noting the use of the words 'fill, still, and will' Paulin argues that 'ill' 'lurks' within them and that this signals unease and even fear of death. Within my last sentence are the words 'hat', 'his', 'ear' and 'eat', but that has absolutely no coded significance. The problem is that Paulin wants to make almost every image in the poem fit his very specific political reading and this just seems contrived. However, the idea that Keats' poem has a political dimension, that by writing about nature he is also writing about his own liberal ideology is certainly an interesting and credible one. We will return to it later in this essay.

Among other qualities, Keats' poetry is celebrated, and sometimes criticised, for its luxuriant sensory overload. To help appreciate this, try reading the opening stanza with the adjectives and adjectival phrases removed:

'Season of mists and fruitfulness,
Friend of the sun,
Conspiring with him how to load and bless
With fruit the vines that round the eves run.
To bend with apples the trees,
And fill all fruit with ripeness,
To swell the gourd, and plump the hazel shells,
With a kernel; to set budding more
And still more flowers for the bees,
Until they think days will never cease,
For Summer has o'er-brimm'd their cells.'

Without reading the original, try adding a sprinkling of adjectives. If you need a bit of help, here's a list: 'mellow'; 'close'; 'bosom'; 'maturing'; 'thatch'; 'moss'd'; 'cottage'; 'to the core'; 'sweet'; 'later'; 'warm'; 'clammy'. That's more than one adjective per line - certainly a liberal sprinkling. Of course, the lush richness isn't generated by the adjectives alone, imagery and Keats' sonic devices are also crucial ingredients.

The imagery in this opening stanza is all about things growing fatter, fuller and riper: The fruit is filled with ripeness; apple trees are so loaded that their branches 'bend'; gourds 'swell', hazels shells are made 'plump', everything is 'budding more/ and still more'; summer hasn't just filled up her stores, they have been filled to spilling, 'oe'r-brimm'd'. Everywhere is plenty, nature's bounty, excess even, fecundity. Keats' imagery also appeals to a wide range of senses. Visual images, such as of the 'maturing sun' and 'vines', mix with tactile ones, such the 'clammy' bees' cells, and with lines that appeal to taste, such as the 'sweet kernel'. And stirring these together Keats creates an intense musicality in his verse. In the first two lines, for example, sibilance combines with assonance and alliteration:

'**Seas**ONs of *m*ist and *m*ellow fruitfuln**ess**,
Clo**se** bos̲OM-*f*riend of the *m*aturing **s**Un.'

The sibilance and long, open 'ee' sounds of 'season' are laced through the whole of the first stanza. Their combined sound runs, for instance, through 'eves' to 'trees' and on to 'sweet' and 'bees' to 'cease' and appears prominently in three end rhymes.

Like a gleaner

Addressing 'her' directly, in the second stanza Keats personifies autumn as a sort of pagan goddess. For a goddess, she's found, however, not in heavenly palaces but in very ordinary agricultural places, such as 'a granary floor'. For a goddess, she's also not remote in any way and she doesn't appear to have favourites, or a priesthood - 'whoever seeks abroad may find' her. She's also a very chilled seeming goddess, as presumably 'careless' means without cares. Further evidence for her  untroubled tranquility is that she can be found 'fast asleep', intoxicated it seems by 'the fume of poppies'. Evidently, she's also not terribly industrious, leaving off her tasks to have a nice midday nap. Hence the 'furrow' remains only 'half-reap'd' and her 'hook' has spared the 'next swath' of flowers. Oddly, she sometimes likes to lie like a human/goddess bridge across a stream, or perhaps rather this image suggests she crosses a brook steadily. She also enjoys watching cider being made, presumably in anticipation of trying a glass or two of the fruity nectar. As in the first stanza, Keats creates a sonically intense texture, especially in the last line. Compare for instance, 'you watch the last oozings by the hour', which has the same overt sense, but none of the rich, lush syrupy music of Keats.

Tom Paulin's comments on the personification of autumn are helpful and interesting. Paulin argues that the use of a 'gleaner', rather than another synonym for a farm-hand or agricultural labourer, is politically significant because a gleaner was 'a member of the rural poor...who has scraped up the grains of corn left after the farm labourers had gathered in the harvest.' Moreover, 'gleaning was made illegal in 1818'. 'By personifying autumn as a gleaner [the poet] is characterising the season as a proud and dignified young woman'. Keats' goddess is a rather humble, agricultural one and, as the first stanza shows, she is generous and her bounty is life-sustaining. Hence, by making a gleaner a goddess, the poet is showing his respect, solidarity with, and veneration for the working poor.

Keats was a second-generation Romantic poet. Like many of the Romantics, his radical aesthetic principles were aligned with his political radicalism. In particular, Keats held politically liberal sympathies and had liberal friends, such as the poet and publisher, Leigh Hunt. Like Hunt, Keats criticised monarchy and protested against social injustice. Like Hunt, he was subject to politically motivated, excoriating reviews. Unlike Hunt, Keats was, however, never imprisoned for his radicalism. By celebrating nature over culture, Keats reveals a political as well as aesthetic orientation. He rejects the urban and the sophisticated and the wealthy and the upper classes; his appreciation of beauty is centred squarely on what is free to all of us, the natural world. His embodiment of this beauty is an ordinary peasant woman, whose work had been criminalised.

Easeful death

Many critics have noted the change in tone in the final stanza of *To Autumn*. Broadly speaking, the first stanza presented the positive aspects of late summer, the second focuses on autumn as a goddess and the last moves into more elegiac mood. Light, for instance, is leaving the landscape, so that the day is 'soft-dying'. The wind, a traditional symbol of animation and imagination grows inconstant, it 'lives or dies'. A choir of gnats are said to 'mourn / among the river sallows'. The final image, of swallows, gathering in the sky suggests departure and draws on classical poetic convention: Traditionally birds taking off and flying away is a symbol of approaching death.

As darkness begins to fall, the last stanza of Keats's ode is dominated by sonic imagery, the music of autumn. As well as the choir of gnats, lambs 'bleat',

crickets 'sing', a robin 'whistles' and the swallows 'twitter'. These noises are not clamorous or discordant; there doesn't seem to be any great resistance to, or unhappiness about, the onward march of time and the consequent intimations of mortality. Like the gnats, it seems the poet is content to be 'borne aloft' or to 'sink' by the 'light wind' of fate. This tranquil mood of acceptance recalls lines from Keats's *Ode to a Nightingale*: '...for many a time / I have been half in love with easeful death'. As with the sensory sensuality of Keats' poems, some critics have objected to this sentiment, arguing that it is unhealthy or unmanly or decadent. What they fail to acknowledge is the active will and force of imagination of the poet who orchestrates this material into beautifully composed verse; an act of creative, shaping and artistic will to set against the poem's overt sentiments. And was it really surprising that a medically trained poet, one who had nursed his younger brother through his fatal consumption and who knew when he himself coughed up blood that it was arterial and therefore his own death sentence, that he was most in love with beauty that is the verge of being lost? For Keats, beauty was made even more beautiful by being transient, at its most radiant in the moments before it gave in to decay. He is intoxicated by the final 'bloom' and 'rosy hue' of the 'soft-dying day' on the 'stubble-plains' [surely an image suggesting the last moments of life leaving a human face]. This is not some decadent aesthetic affectation, but the real lived experience of a poet who was dead by the age of just 25.

To Autumn distilled:

FRUITFULNESS - SUN - BLESS - VINES - APPLES - RIPENESS - PLUMP - BUDDING - FLOWERS - NEVER - OE'R-BRIMMED - OFT - WHOEVER - GRANARY - SOFT-LIFTED - ASLEEP - DROWS'D - SPARES - GLEANER - BROOK - PATIENT - OOZINGS - SONGS - MUSIC - SOFT-DYING - ROSY - WAILFUL - BORNE - WIND - BLEAT - SING - WHISTLES - SWALLOWS

William Wordsworth, *Composed Upon Westminster Bridge*

Nothing to show more fair

From the ringing declarative first line, 'earth has nothing to show more fair' onwards, in this sonnet Wordsworth rhapsodises about London, comparing its majesty and beauty to monumental features of the natural world, such as valleys and hills, describing the arresting impact of this beauty on his 'soul' so that the poet is so moved he cries out 'Dear God!'. The tone is enraptured, the style increasingly exclamatory [notice the three exclamation marks in the sestet] the imagery glittering. Wordsworth's vision of London is of an extraordinarily beautiful, peaceful, almost unearthly city; a sleeping, harmonious and majestic city - a Romantic vision of heaven. Crucially there are no people in this picturesque dawn scene. The magical moment of utter stillness and tranquility hasn't yet been destroyed by the noisy, unruly masses who will soon wake and fill the teeming London streets. Produced a decade or so earlier, William Blake's depiction of the city in his poem *London* was written from a street-level perspective. Blake, of course, was a Londoner, born and bred, and spent most of his life in the city. His poem is written from in and amongst the city's inhabitants and focuses on the corrupting impact of the city on its populace. As a visitor, Wordsworth doesn't present a view from within the city, but from above it, up on a bridge, detached from the grimy reality, looking down upon it.

Shadows and light

Hovering somewhere in the background, shadowing the poem's radiant vision, is another city, Paris, and another country, France. When the French Revolution had broken out in 1789 Wordsworth was exhilarated, writing, 'joy was it then to be alive, to be young was a very heaven'. Indeed, he travelled to France to support the cause. By 1792 hopes for a better society had, however, been swept away on a rising tide of blood and violence. British radicals, including Wordsworth, had hoped revolution would usher in a new fairer, more democratic society. The bitter reality was that one form of tyranny was replaced by another. In the streets of Paris over a thousand people had been slaughtered in the 1790s during the period known as The Terror. Afraid that the revolutionary fire would spread to England, the British government clamped down hard on political radicals. For Wordsworth, London [and England] in 1802 - calm, peaceful, free - appeared to be everything Paris [and France] was not.

London, Wordsworth tells us is 'fair', as fair as anything on 'earth'. In similar superlative mode, he says that 'never' has the sun lit more beautifully a scene than this. The poet tells us the city is also majestical and 'touching'. He personifies London as a deity, wearing 'the beauty of the morning' like an elegant 'garment' [garments can, however, be removed, which might signal that the beauty is only a superficial effect created by the hopeful morning sun]. This powerful single entity has a 'mighty heart', suggesting strength, courage and goodness. Like a jewel, the city also shines; it is 'bright and glittering'. Surprisingly, considering the industrial revolution was beginning to pick up pace, there is no pollution; the city air is 'smokeless'. Moreover, there is a sense of universal calmness 'so deep' and all the features of the city are 'open', unguarded, with no need of protection. The notoriously smelly and polluted Thames is described as moving with a gentle, graceful motion, 'glideth', the sense of ease enhanced by the archaic verb form. The river Blake had described as 'chartered', Wordsworth personifies [in opposite terms] as following 'his own sweet will', able to do exactly what it wants. Fair, open, calm, beautiful, free, London, at least this morning moment touched by the sun's warming light, seems the perfect city. Perhaps London is also a metonym; as the capital city it stands in here for England as a whole. Perhaps, in appreciating in a new, deeper sense the qualities of London, Wordsworth is aligning himself too with England and moving away from his youthful infatuation with revolutionary France. Certainly, this sonnet expresses the power of a place to affect our feelings, as well as the power of our feelings to transform how we see a place.

There's a more personal layer to the context of this poem too. Wordsworth wrote *Composed Upon Westminster Bridge* as he travelled from London to Calais to meet with the French woman with whom he had a relationship nearly ten years earlier. The young poet hoped to come to some sort of financial understanding with this woman so that he could be freed to marry his childhood sweetheart, Mary Hutchinson. Some of the tension and excitement of that anticipated meeting, where he would meet his nine-year-old illegitimate daughter for the first time, and some of the feeling of being on the verge of potentially momentous change is woven into the fabric of a poem that finishes before the city actually awakes and the new day begins.

Harmonious form

Composed Upon Westminster Bridge is a Petrarchan or Italian sonnet. The word sonnet is derived from the Italian for 'little song' and was usually used to express and explore the nature of love, especially in the Elizabethan period. Here Wordsworth uses the form to show his intense emotional response to the scene [the poem could be read as a love song to London] a trope typical in Romantic poetry. The elegant compactness of the sonnet is also ideally suited to the 'snapshot' depiction of the city.

One of the major technical challenges of writing a Petrarchan sonnet in English is the fact that the poem can only use four or five rhyme sounds. This restriction was one of the reasons why English poets, notably Shakespeare, introduced more rhymes into the sonnet form. In fact, Wordsworth chooses the most demanding version of a Petrarchan sonnet, composing the whole poem with just four rhymes:

1. 'fair'/ 'wear'/ 'bare'/ 'air'
2. 'by'/ 'majesty'/ 'lie'/ 'sky'
3. 'hill'/ 'will'/ 'still'
4. 'steep'/ 'deep'/ 'asleep'

Such technical virtuosity creates a sense of sonic harmony, order and balance, so that the sonnet in its construction embodies the qualities of the scene it celebrates. The sense of unity is enhanced by the absence of a volta, or turn in the sonnet after the octave. Conventionally the two stanzas in a sonnet, the octave and sestet, have a question and answer, call and response relationship. Conventionally something proposed in the octave is answered by the sestet. In this poem, however, there is no counter argument or different perspective opened up in the sestet. Instead the poem progresses seamlessly onwards with further lavish praise.

That said, Wordsworth must have been aware of the unsettling double meanings in play in the final, concluding line. The adjective 'still', for instance, can refer to time or to a lack of movement. More significantly, 'lying' obviously has another meaning underneath the one Wordsworth seems to be employing. Intentionally or unintentionally, the penultimate word of the poem may make us reflect on the extent to which the picture of London that the poet paints may be just a romantic illusion. A spell-like illusion that will be broken as soon as the slumbering city awakes.

Composed upon Westminster Bridge distilled:

EARTH – SOUL – MAJESTY – GARMENT – BEAUTY – TEMPLES – OPEN – GLITTERING – NEVER – SPLENDOUR – CALM – WILL – GOD - LYING

William Blake, *London*

The first thing to notice about Blake's poem is its burning anger. Written over two hundred years ago, the nightmare vision of this poem still seems irradiated with the poet's righteous fury. Fury at the corruption London's inhabitants had to endure, fury at the powers maintaining and enforcing this corruption. And who or what is to blame for the universal corruption? Blake is characteristically direct and bold: The finger of blame is pointed directly, unwaveringly at commerce, the church and the monarchy.

Land and water in this poem have both been 'chartered', an adjective that indicates that they have become property, to be bought and sold by chartered companies. However, Blake subtly implies a potential counter force; the verb 'flows', with its slight echo of 'wander', perhaps implies that the river at least has the potential to escape its commercial restriction. For Blake, the Church of England was part of a corrupt, oppressive state. Here the churches are 'black'ning' because they should be an active voice of protest against the exploitation of children. The failure of the church blackens its name, an idea made tangible by the blackening of its bricks. The blood of the soldier runs down the palace walls - a gruesome symbol of the sacrifice the ordinary man makes for King and country.

Every voice

Repetition is a key poetic device for all poets, but it is especially important for Blake. It can fall into a few different categories: diction [aka vocabulary]; syntax [word order]; images and sounds.

- In *London* there are lots of 'ins', 'ands', 'everys' as well as 'chartered', 'marks' and 'cry'.
- As well as repetition of single words there is repetition of syntax: 'in every...in every...in every'.
- Sound patterns are also repeated, such as in 'marks of weakness, marks of woe', 'mind-forg'd manacles', 'most through midnight', 'blasts' and 'blights'.
- Most importantly, images are also repeated: The images of the chimney sweep, the soldier and the prostitute are essentially three versions of the same figure; the isolated character marginalized and exploited by society.

As well as creating rhetorical emphasis and a powerful rhythmical charge, reminiscent of spells and incantations, the poem's insistent repetition creates an almost claustrophobic sound world, one that is an aural equivalent of the oppression Blake is describing.

The poem's rhyme scheme is cross-rhyme in quatrains: ABAB, CDCD and so forth. All the rhymes are masculine, a choice that also contributes to the peculiar intensity of the poem. For example, in the fourth line the stress starts with a strong stress on 'marks' and ends with another strong stress on 'woe'. Each stanza constitutes one sentence, completed in its final emphatic monosyllable. Metre, rhyme, diction, lineation and syntax all work together to amass maximum weight and stress on these last key words, 'woe', 'hear', 'walls' and finally, of course, 'hearse'.

The poem comprises four stanzas of four lines [quatrains] each with four beats. This consistency creates a concentration, further adding to its forcefulness. Structurally the poem also increases in intensity, as we move from verbs such as 'flow' and 'mark' in the first stanza to the more powerful emphatic 'curse', 'blasts' and 'blights' in the final stanza. As we will go on to examine, this pattern is re-enforced by the increasingly poignant examples of exploitation, from the general populace, to the chimney sweeper, to the 'youthful harlot' whose curse Blake hears 'most'.

The dark mark

As in fellow poet William Wordsworth's famous 'I wander lonely as a cloud', 'wander' is a form of motion particularly associated with Romanticism. Wandering suggests freedom, finding one's own path, without any specific aim in mind. It may also imply a sense of being lost. In Blake's poem, the verb emphasizes the idea that exploitation in London is universal; the poet doesn't have to search for it, whatever direction he takes he's sure to find it. Though they are in the active voice, the verbs connected to the narrator – 'wander', 'mark', 'hear' - suggest that Blake is passive and perhaps powerless. Rather than an active participant in the world of the poem who can make things happen, he is an outsider, a sympathetic witness, registering his impressions as vividly as he can. Perhaps this is the role of the artist.

However, look at the line: 'and mark in every face I meet/ marks of weakness, marks of woe'. 'Mark' is used here first as a verb and then as a noun, and is a word connecting the narrator to the suffering people. Blake could easily have chosen a different verb. He was an engraver as well as a poet and to engrave the pictures that accompanied the poems in *Songs of Innocence and Experience* he would have had to cut into metal. Compared to 'see' or 'notice', 'mark' signals permanence. It also implies something doomed, as in the mark of Cain, or for Harry Potter fans the 'dark mark'. The fact that the poet 'marks' the people's 'marks' implies an equality and connection between them. If he is an outsider, he's an insider too, expressing a radical empathy with the suffering he witnesses.

Repetition of the adjective 'every' emphasizes Blake's idea that every human being matters. The crowd represents the ordinary masses, the common people, whose suffering is often ignored by those in power. Over in France, Europe's leaders had witnessed the first 'successful' rebellion of the commoners in history. The British government responded with a harsh crackdown on freedom. Romantic poets often sided with people marginalised by society or oppressed by authority; Blake's poem protests against the often malign effects of power on those at the bottom of society. The soldier, sweep and prostitute are emblems of exploitation: The sweep would have been a young boy sold into a form of slavery [see Blake's two Chimney Sweeper poems in *Songs of Innocence and Experience*]. Abused and brutalised, sweeps were regarded at this time as the lowest form of human life, on a par with 'savages' who shared their black skin. The soldier's blood is used to protect the state and the monarchy. The prostitute is, however, an example of the worst possible exploitation. Blake believed love to be sacred. Turning sex and love into a commodity to be bought and sold was therefore a sin against God, the most heinous form of sacrilege.

This is a poem full of aural as well as visual imagery: The voices of the Londoners, the clink of their mental manacles, the cries of the sweepers, the cursing of the prostitute. For Romantic Poets, such as Blake, nature was sacred. Nature manifested God on earth and was a great source of poetic inspiration. This unhappy, discordant, diseased, corrupted city is the nightmare

opposite of Eden, an anti-pastoral. The image of the soldier's 'sigh' running in 'blood down palace walls' combines sound with sight. It is extraordinary in two ways: firstly, Blake transforms sound, a 'sigh', into something visual. The synaesthetic effect generated has a nightmarish quality;

secondly, as we have already noted, he firmly directs the blame at the King. This was a very dangerous thing to say in England in 1792, in a time when some of Blake's fellow radicals were being arrested by the government and attacked by pro monarchy gangs. The penalties for treason were very severe.

Thought control

The 'mind forg'd manacles' is one of Blake's most celebrated images. It is characteristically Blakean because it conveys an idea [here of being brainwashed] in a concrete, physical image. The image of the manacles is one of mental chains, thought control, indoctrination. The poet does not indicate who forges these manacles. It could be that they are made by the state through propaganda. But they could also be formed in the minds of individuals, in their blinkered perceptions and ways of seeing the world. In either case, there is hope - these aren't real chains; they are 'mind forg'd' and perceptions can be changed, perhaps by poetry. 'Forg'd' is a doubly appropriate verb: An image drawn from metal work, it is a pun. These perceptions of reality are forgeries, forgeries that can and must be exposed by the sort of truth articulated in this poem.

Arguably, however, the poem's most potent image is the final one. Notice how the structure of the poem develops in a cinematic fashion. Starting with the equivalent of an establishing shot - a wide-angle image of the landscape, the focus narrows to a closer in inspection of the crowds and finishes with a shot of a single emblematic figure. Like a film camera we sweep the whole scene then zoom in as day darkens to night, before finishing, seemingly inevitably at the apex of exploitation, the moral midnight of the 'youthful harlot'.

Blake employs an image of sexual infection as a metaphor for moral corruption. Disease spreads through time and space: It will be spread through the generations, from the prostitute to her child; spread from prostitute to client, and spread into marriage, the home, the family. The deadly destruction this process will wreak is conveyed by those violent plosive & alliterative verbs 'blasts' and the biblical 'blights', and through the similarly biblical word 'plagues'. Plagues also suggests disease and especially the deadly Black Plague. Hence Blake evokes the image of God's punishment of sin. As the image of the charming plague doctor at the start of this essay suggests, it's like something out of *Night of the Living Dead*. Corruption so potent can, indeed, even transform a celebration of new life into an image of death, as in the startling oxymoron of the 'marriage hearse'.

Songs of Innocence and Experience

London is from *Songs of Experience* [1792], the companion piece to his earlier *Songs of Innocence*. Blake was an idealist who wanted to see a better, fairer, kinder world. The front covers signal the different tones of the two books; where the Innocence image is maternal and comforting, the Experience image is sombre and suggests mourning for a spiritual loss. In many of the Experience poems Blake analyses and criticizes the harsh values of his society. Throughout the collection, he protests against injustice and exploitation. He stands up as a champion of the poor and challenges the cruelty of those in power. In this enterprise, Blake's spiritual guide was Christ who he called 'Jesus, the imagination'. An artist,  engraver and a poet, Blake illustrated his poems with designs that were integral to the overall effect. Many of the illustrations accompanying the *Innocence* poems are rich, boldly-coloured, sensual designs, presenting children playing in harmonious relation within exuberantly fertile images of nature. In contrast, the palette of the *Experience* is much narrower and gloomier, conjuring a shadow world, drained of colour, dominated by greys and blacks.

The characters in these images express suffering and misery. Boxed in by the borders of the page, they appear trapped in their oppressive worlds. It is interesting that Blake depicts himself as two figures in the illustration to *London*. He is both the angelic child guide and the old man being lead through the circles of this particular depiction of hell. In other words, he is both innocence and experience. Significantly at the end of the poem the image of innocence has disappeared.

An age of revolutions

Blake's *Songs of Innocence* poems generally focus on childhood and are celebratory and optimistic in tone; the 'Experience' poems are much angrier. This darkening of mood between the two may have been due to Blake's reaction to the French Revolution of 1789. Like other Romantic poets, initially Blake saw the revolution as a great uprising of the human spirit, a liberation of the masses from the corrupt and unjust powers of the State. But as time went on news filtered through to England of appalling massacres carried out by the revolutionary forces. Over time it was becoming apparent that the French Revolution would result in one form of tyranny, that of the Monarchy, being replaced by another, that of the Masses.

London crunched:

WANDER – CHARTERED – MARK – WOE – EVERY – CRY – EVERY – MANACLES – CHIMNEY-SWEEPER – CHURCH – SOLDIER – PALACE – MIDNIGHT – HARLOT – NEW-BORN – HEARSE.

Emily Dickinson, *I started Early - Took my Dog*

Telling it *slant*

There's several peculiar things about Dickinson's poetry and this curious, magical poem in particular. If you didn't know anything about Dickinson's poetry, the title might lead you to expect a nice little ditty about a country walk with a beloved pet, or some such light material. If you set off with this sort of expectation, the poem swiftly takes you somewhere much stranger and far

more surreal, a place where 'frigates' [which could be either boats or perhaps birds] have 'hands', and thoughts, thoughts that allow them to make bizarre presumptions, such as mistaking the poem's human narrator for a 'mouse', a mouse who appears to have run 'aground', like a beached boat, from

a sea that has a 'basement' and 'upper floor', like a building. However, putting the surreal, protean imagery aside for a moment, the most obvious examples of the oddities that so bamboozled Emily Dickinson's first readers are her use of capital letters and dashes or hyphens [we'll call them dashes in the rest of this essay]. If you're a teacher, to help highlight these distinctive features, you could present the poem first to a class with them removed, only revealing

Dickinson's eccentricities after the poem has been analysed. That way you can explore whether these features are mere curious adornments or whether they are more fundamental to the poem's meanings and effects.

'I started early, took my dog,
And visited the sea,
The mermaids in the basement
Came out to look at me'

[and so forth]

When the first publishers of Emily Dickinson's work came across her poems and their idiosyncrasies their instinct was to 'correct' them. They did this by straightening the poems out, tidying them up, giving them titles, punctuating them more conventionally and even by squeezing their typically gaunt forms into more familiar shapes. Only over time did readers come to realise that an essential part of this poet's artistic genius lay exactly in her unconventionality, and that her idiosyncrasies - most particularly a taste for dashes - were fundamental aspects of this originality. Not that there were, in fact, many publishers. During her lifetime [1830-1886] only about ten of Dickinson's poems were published. However, after the poet's death, her sister discovered a box containing numerous volumes full of poems. Over time, nearly two thousand poems, which had been carefully hand stitched into little books, began to be published. And slowly Dickinson's reputation grew, and grew. So much so that nowadays this famously reclusive poet is considered to be one of America's greatest poets and a major feminist literary icon.

The woman in white

Emily Dickinson lived almost her entire life in small town called Amherst in Massachusetts. Moreover, from her early twenties onwards Dickinson lived as a recluse, only rarely leaving her house or receiving visitors. Literary scholars are not certain about the causes of her withdrawal from the outside world, but the consensus is that the poet fell in love, probably with an older, married preacher called Charles Wadsworth. Though she shared some precious time with Wadsworth, it seems her love was not requited. Soon after moved far away Dickinson became a recluse, hardly seeing any visitors and dressing always in a white dress. In her letters from around this time the poet also wrote that she 'had a terror' that may have precipitated some sort of breakdown. The relation between unrequited love and the 'terror' isn't clear. Other scholars, especially critics reading the poet through a feminist perspective, argue that Dickinson consciously withdrew from the outside world because she felt alienated by its attitudes and behaviour. Whether her withdrawal was a rational decision, whether it was triggered by rejection in love or by some kind of existential terror, or a combination of the above, we do not know. We do know she faced some sort of crisis and after this became a recluse. We also know that images of entrapment within confined, coffin-like spaces occur frequently in her poetry. And we also know that the coast is around 90 miles away from Amherst and it's unlikely Dickinson would have visited it often, if at all.

Dreaming of transformation

Certainly, Dickinson's depiction of a beach seems to be generated more through her imagination than through any direct observation of geographical or botanical features. This is a beach, after all, boasting fabulous creatures such as mermaids. It's a beach and seascape that's also alarmingly unfamiliar to us. Not only does it have mermaids, but, as we've already pointed out, the sea is presented as if it is a house with a 'basement' and an 'upper floor', collapsing the essential distinction between land and sea. Nothing is how we expect it to be in Dickinson's dream-like poem-world and things rapidly get stranger: Frigates extending 'hempen hands' suggests nets cast down from the surface - a striking enough image - but, more peculiarly, they do this because they mistakenly presume the speaker is a 'mouse' that has run 'aground'. That's not an obvious thing for any boat to think or for a mouse to do.

The following 'but' at the start of the third stanza is also surprising. Perhaps Dickinson is implying that powerful, masculine forces on the 'upper floor' [i.e. above the fantastical female ones in the 'basement'], symbolised by the frigates, mistakenly assume her to be a small, vulnerable woman, like a 'mouse' and in need of help, run 'aground'. Hence 'no Man moved Me'. The speaker is stronger, more independent and more resolute than others, especially male others suppose, perhaps. Stoically she seems to allow the tide to come in, rise up and cover where she stands. This tide is also a masculine force. However, where the mermaids just observed and the frigates tried to help, the force of the sea is overwhelming and threatening, even predatory: 'made as He would eat me up'.

There is something oddly fairy-tale or nursery-rhyme like about this poem, with

its mermaids, sea-house, boats with hands, shoe and apron, dog and mouse and later a 'silver heel'. The simplicity of the run of conjunctions placed emphatically at the starts of lines [eight 'ands', a 'but' and an 'until'] adds to this impression. The personified sea is also rather like the wolf from Little Red Riding Hood, with the speaker's passivity - she allows the sea to simply go 'past' the barriers of her clothes - analogous to the little girl in the fairy tale's culpability in her own undoing. The image of the sea as a potent male forceT, sweeping over the defences and consuming a solitary female also recalls Greek myths of sea-Gods, the shape-shifting Proteus and the King-of-the-Seas, Poseidon.

Dickinson's image of obliteration of the self is characteristically brilliant and disorientating. The speaker fears being eaten up 'as wholly as Dew/ Upon a dandelion's sleeve'. Just as the world around the speaker seems unfamiliar, shape-shifting and dream-like, so too, is the poet's depiction of herself in the poem[2]. At first she seems an ordinary person with a dog going for a walk. Then she compares herself to a 'mouse'. Later she is as insubstantial, fluid, delicate

---

[2] Presenting the self in this sort of unstable, even fractured manner is typical of Dickinson's work and is often identified as one of its 'ahead-of-its-time', pre-modernist features. In *The Cambridge Companion to Emily Dickinson* Wendy Martin notes how the poet uses 'strategies of disorientation' to 'unsettle the reader' and convey 'identities that are always unstable, always in process' [p.6], while Daneen Wardop observes that 'the experience of disjunctive identity, one of the hallmarks of modernism and postmodernism, is an area Dickinson pioneered'. [p.142]

and temporary as the 'dew' that awaits inevitable evaporation by the sun. By analogy the sea is being compared to the sun and water to heat, and the speaker thinks of herself as a tiny piece of water! As with the sea and the land, essential distinctions between things seem to collapse and blur in the poem's hazy, dream-like logic. Then the speaker seems to suddenly awaken from her dreamy, blurry impassivity to the imminent danger, 'then - I started - too' and she flees back towards the 'Solid Town'. The sea has been just 'the Sea', but also a building, a predatory male and like the sun, and now he/ it has developed legs and wears a 'Silver Heel' [a fairy tale image, as we've noted]. Pursuing the speaker 'close behind', almost touching her 'ankle', when the sea-God-predatory-male-creature realises he/it is out-of-place on unfamiliar territory it acts in courtly, even princely fashion, 'bowing' and with a 'Mighty look' gallantly withdrawing.

And what happened to the poor dog, we might ask? Did it make it back to the town or not? We'll never know, of course, because, like Immortality in another famous Dickinson poem, after the first stanza it doesn't get another look in for the rest of the poem. As  the only witness to all these rather peculiar events, if it could talk, the dog might have a rather interesting story to tell. Perhaps students could even re-write the poem as a shaggy dog story...

Fear and desire at the seaside

Like Dickinson, let's put the dog to one side, and consider the significance of the poem. What does this strange story actually mean, do you think? In Dickinson's poems as a whole, and within individual examples, there is often a tension between entrapment and liberation. *I started Early* seems to me to express the poet's longing for liberation, but also her deep fear of freedom. Visiting the sea is clearly a form of escape, from both an interior space and from surrounding society. There's a Romantic element here - the individual self escaping to nature and finding therein beauty, truth and inspiration. However, for Dickinson the interaction with nature has a very different effect. She may let the tide wash over her - an image of total immersion in the forces of nature suggesting at some level her desire to at one with nature - but quickly this interaction becomes threatening. The poet fears obliteration of her identity by the overmastering male force of nature, symbolised in turn by drowning, being consumed and by her comparison of herself to 'dew'. Undoubtedly there is a sexual dimension to the speaker's desires - the sea passes up her body, over her defences, and being eaten can symbolise fears of sexual intercourse [see, for multiple examples Angela Carter's *The Bloody Chamber*]. In addition, there is the startling image of the speaker's shoes overflowing with 'Pearl'. This metaphor works on several levels. Firstly, it implies that beautiful or perhaps wise things, such as this poem, may come, but only at a great price or from something ugly. Secondly, the image works visually as an analogue for frothy surf following the speaker up the beach. And it is in that second sense that the image of 'pearl' filling up the poet's shoe that has a sexual component.

Aspects of form

Characteristically Dickinson uses the hymn or ballad form for her poems, lending them both a religious dimension and an organisational solidity that act as bulwarks against the often fractured and unsettling contents within. As many readers have pointed out, her poems can be sung to the tune of *Amazing Grace*. The stanza form is quatrains, with alternating lines of tetrameter and trimeter, cross-rhymed on the second and fourth lines. The poet only deviates from the regular pattern in the fourth stanza where the 'oo' rhymed is carried from the previous stanza to do its bit in generating a sense of suspended animation or the trance-like state that renders the speaker immobile for a while,  and in the final stanzas, where both 'heel/ pearl' and 'know/ withdrew' are half-rhymes. The transition from the full rhymes of the first four stanzas to these half-rhymes adds to the unsettling feeling of disturbance.

Earlier in this essay we asked whether Dickinson's liberal use of dashes were merely decorative of whether they serve any greater purpose. In addition to their ornamental effect, they appear to serve three main purposes:

1. They slow the reader down and indicate points at which to pause, to bring out the dramatic effect. This is most prominent in lines such as 'and then - I started - too - ' which generates a staccato pattern, conveying the speaker's hesitation and uncertainty.

2. Scan the whole poem and you'll see dashes are the only punctuation used. Grammatically, dashes are rather indeterminate - they can work like commas, brackets, even as full stops. There's something a bit skittish and unsettled about them, especially when they're employed so liberally as in this poem.

3. Dashes also perform two opposite functions - they separate, as in the adverbial phrase ' - upon the sands - ', but they also connect. Over half the lines in this poem end with a dash and every single stanza finishes with one. Visually the right-hand side of each dash connects only to the white space at the side of the page, as if trying to link to something either not there or invisible. The effect is especially striking in the final line of the poem which finishes with a dash after 'withdrew', connecting that word and the entire poem to endless nothingness and silence. Rather than closure, the poem ends open-endedly, with incompleteness.

In summary, *I started Early* expresses the poet's desire for freedom and interaction with greater, transforming natural powers beyond the confines of her immediate experience. Perhaps the powerful masculine force of the sea is a poetic embodiment of Charles Wadsworth and the way he swept Dickinson off her feet, but then later withdrew his attentions. Or perhaps it embodies mortality, the ultimate force that will consume the self. Certainly, the speaker is conflicted by her imaginative visit to the sea, inspired, but also frightened by the potential for liberation and what that freedom might entail.

Crunching the poem by just picking out the capitalised words gives us:

EARLY - TOOK - DOG - SEA - MERMAIDS - BASEMENT - CAME

- FRIGATES - HEMPEN - HANDS - PRESUMING - ME - MOUSE - SANDS - MAN - ME - TIDE - SHOE - APRON - BODICE - HE - DEW - DANDELION'S SLEEVE - HE - HE - SILVER HEEL - ANKLE - SHOES - PEARL - WE - SOLID TOWN - ONE - HE - MIGHTY - THE - SEA -

Thomas Hardy, *Where the Picnic Was*

Less is more

'Grandiloquence' is a word sometimes associated with Victorian literature and Victorian poetry especially. It means language that is extravagant, designed to impress, rather puffed up and pompous. A grandiloquent poem is one in which the diction and phrasing have been inflated, as if by over-vigorous working of a bicycle pump and varnished by over-vigorous application of elbow grease. In contrast, plain and spare, Hardy's style in his Edwardian lyric poem, *Where the Picnic Was*, is the polar opposite. Language, especially language in poetry, doesn't get much starker, plainer or more down-to-earth than this. Emotionally and tonally, the poem is very understated. Hardy doesn't really tell us how he feels, but he gives the reader enough information for us to fill in the emotional blanks, as, hopefully, we shall see.

The poem is more like a simple sketch than a painting. Hardy was, of course, a great novelist and he sketches the outlines of this story and its situation in a series of swift strokes, with minimal fuss: The season is winter, the weather poor and cold, the landscape grey, the speaker is climbing a hill, returning to a familiar spot. Finding the remains of their picnic fire he reflects on his solitariness now, his previous companions having either 'wandered far' or died.

Simple truth, miscalled simplicity

The language used in his poem is universally plain and simple. It's simple in terms of the vocabulary, how this vocabulary is employed and also in terms of how the words are combined and arranged through syntax. Many of the lines, for example, are composed entirely of basic, common monosyllabic words, mostly of Anglo-Saxon origin:

'Where we made the fire';   'one the hill to the sea';
'and scan and trace';   'now a cold wind blows'
'yes, I am here';   'and one – has shut her eyes'.

In fact, over half the lines, 16/30 are made up entirely of monosyllables. There are only two trisyllables – 'forsaken' and 'evermore'- and very few, if any, words unfamiliar to any competent reader. Indeed, there's little in the poem's diction or phrasing to betray its Victorian or Edwardian context. Perhaps the use of 'aye' and the archaic sounding, 'sward'; at a push, perhaps, 'whereon'. Other than those examples, the language seems modern and stripped back, almost to the bare bones. Hardy avoids using any long, fancy words. His vocabulary is also predominantly Anglo-Saxon – he avoids words with Greek, Latin or Romance language origins.

Simple, everyday words can, however, be used in complex, symbolic ways. A good example is the opening lines of Blake's *The Sick Rose*, 'O rose thou are sick', where the pronoun and the reference to illness bring multiple symbolic dimensions into play. With the possible exception of the 'burnt circle', Hardy eschews any complex symbolism or figurative imagery. Okay, we could argue that climbing a hill and the 'cold wind' carry a little symbolism, but these are common symbols that require no effort of interpretation.

The poet also puts the common, familiar words together in common, familiar ways, so that the poem sounds like slightly heightened speech: 'Yes, I am here/ Just as last year'. Eschewing the usual poetic devices, such as figurative imagery, symbolism and sonic effects, keeping the language pared-down, plain and simple, arranging it in straightforward syntax, how does Hardy make his poem powerful and poignant? Firstly, the poem conveys an experience with which most readers can easily relate. What do you think of when you hear the word 'picnic'? Probably you think of summer, of being with friends or family and of having fun out of doors, perhaps in a beautiful, natural environment. The poem's subject is also loss and loneliness, its central contrast between a happy time in the past and the sad present. Again, this is easy for us to relate to. Secondly, the plain language suits the familiar subject matter and makes the situation easy for us to understand. More than that, and more subtly, the short, almost stunted lines and seemingly matter-of-fact tone, suggest the depth of emotion behind the lines. By writing so starkly, Hardy engages the reader's imagination in completing the sketch he outlines. The effect of the principle of understatement is most obvious and most poignantly evinced in the final two lines. Here death is presented euphemistically, as if it is a gentle thing, like sleep, and a matter of conscious choice:

'And one – has shut her eyes'

One who has shut their eyes, might also be able to open them again, which suggests this state may only be temporary. There is a tenderness and a delicacy here that is the very opposite of mawkishness. The reader has to imagine the feelings that accompany these lines and the emotional impact of the fact that this person has left the speaker 'for evermore'.

An inevitable danger of understatement and of Hardy's sketch-like technique, is that readers might not be able to fill in the gaps or read between the lines. Would it have made the poem more touching if Hardy had been explicit about the dead female being his wife, Emma? I don't think so, because by not making this clear Hardy allows readers to project different interpretations into the gap, personalising their readings. Hence the dead female could be a daughter or sister or even a mother. The point surely is the devastating effect of this loss, after which there seem to be no more words.

However, that said, knowing some of the context of this poem might help to enrich your appreciation. *Where the Picnic Was* was written between 1912 and 1913 as part of a collection of poems responding to the unexpected death of

Hardy's wife, Emma in November 1912. Eventually the poem was placed as the final one in a sequence of poems dealing with the aftermath of Emma's death, so that those last lines accumulate greater weight and resonance. For more information on the biographical background to the poem and explanation of the significance of the other picnickers go to: greatpoetryexplained.blogspot.co.uk/2017/03/where-picnic-was-thomas-hardy.html. There's also a good explanation of the significance of the symbol of the burnt circle in relation to other poems by Hardy from this time.

The Disturbance within

Where the Picnic Was requires the reader to read actively and alertly. In retrospect the 'we' in the first line is, for instance, highly significant, but Hardy ensures we pass over it swiftly in our first reading. The poet draws our attention away by repeating the first word of the title as the first word of the poem, indicating that the location, 'where', is the most important focus for our attention. The trochaic trimeter also serves this purpose. Nevertheless, a reasonably astute reader will still notice the shift from this collective pronoun to the singular 'I' in the first line and realise the significance. Working out the tone and feelings here presents more of a problem. The lines move forward quickly, and there's a terseness that is almost off-hand. The fact that the speaker climbs 'slowly' could, however, imply reluctance, or age, or incapacity. 'Winter mire' suggests a dreary atmosphere and, if we know Hardy's novels, we are likely to recall his fondness for pathetic fallacy, whereby the weather indicates a character's mood. 'Forsaken' is a stronger adjective than we might expect, but this is countered by the casual, unemotional phrase 'quite readily' that concludes the stanza.

Similarly, the poem's form expresses a tension between apparent stolid, matter-of-factness and implied emotional disturbance. For example, superficially, the first two stanzas look solid and regular. Both are nine lines long, have similar line lengths and each has four rhyme sounds. Closer inspection, however, reveals an uneasiness, almost a restlessness within this apparent outer order. Line lengths vary markedly in terms of metre, syllables and number of words. The shortest lines, metrically, are dimeters, such as 'I slowly climb'. In terms of words and syllables, the shortest lines have just two words or four syllables. Longer lines are trimeters and are up to six words with six syllables. Metrically there's no clear pattern either. If the first two lines of the poem are scanned as trochaic trimeters, the third and fifth are certainly iambic and dimeters. Alternatively, the first two lines can be scanned as dimeters - if they are read as beginning with two unstressed feet - making both lines comprised of an anapest followed by an iamb, thus giving them mixed feet and making them different metrically from other lines in the stanza. Then there's the rhyme scheme. Having established a mixed pattern of cross-rhymes and couplets in the first stanza, Hardy shuffles this pattern in the second and, more radically shakes it up in the longer last stanza.

While the first stanza has one couplet, the second has two and the third begins with three in succession, before switching to a type of rhyme pattern seen at the end of Petrarchan sonnets. If such close reading bores you rigid, or leaves you unconvinced, just scan the right-hand side of the poem and you'll notice the unevenness that's shot through the whole construction.

Though, as the title signals, this is a poem about a place, about a 'where', and about how our memories and experiences are intimately connected to places, it is also a poem about the great, unbridgeable gulf between the past and the present, about a then and a now that are radically and irrevocably poles apart. Poles apart that the bereft speaker knows he can never bridge.

Where the Picnic Was crunched:

WE – SUMMER – BRANCH – HILL – I – WINTER – SCAN –
FORSAKEN READILY – COLD – GREY – SHOWS – BURNT –
CHARRED – SWARD – I – RELIC – DAY – YES – LAST – SEA –
STRAIGHT – SAME – FOUR – FAR – FROM – ROAR – NO –
SHUT – EVERMORE

Edward Thomas, *Adlestrop*

Never such innocence again

If there were a top ten for Britain's favourite poems, I expect *Adlestrop* might just make the cut. What is it about this slight, wistful, metrically loose-limbed poem in which nothing much actually happens that has made it so popular and enduring? Certainly, the poem's context plays an important part. Written just six weeks before the outbreak of WWI, *Adlestrop* captures a sense of harmonious and innocent peace - a calm that seemed endless, but all-too-soon would be shattered by the storms of war. Then there's the fact that the poem was written by Edward Thomas, a fine prose writer only recently converted to poetry by his friend Robert Frost. After his death Thomas would be credited for bringing a modern sensibility to Georgian poetry and celebrated as the forefather of modern English verse. Stopped momentarily on his onward journey through life, the speaker is also the Edward Thomas who had not yet decided to enlist in the British army and who had not yet been killed only two years later in the Battle of Arras in 1917, while the first edition of his poems was still in production.

Clearly, reading back down the lens of history, these contexts, socio-historical and biographical, add considerable poignancy to the poem. Looking backwards, there's perhaps a nostalgia for the sort of world and the sort of

65

England that the poem encapsulates. But, arguably, even more than this, it is the themes and experience that the poet outlines and the eloquent and unpretentious way in which he expresses them that make readers connect so strongly to Thomas' poem.

A machine age

Sometimes it seems that modern life is constantly speeding up. There's always more to do than the time to do it in. If we're not busily doing business, we can feel we'll not being productive and grow restless. Boundaries between home and work, or home and school have become blurred, so that when we're at home we're often doing, or thinking about doing, work. The technology we almost all carry and use daily has brought many benefits, of course, but it has also tied us to emails and social media, to Twitter, Facebook and Instagram, so that, anxious that we might be missing something important, we find it hard to disconnect, take time out to unwind and relax. So, too, it must have seemed to Edward Thomas at the start of the twentieth century, at the start of the hustle and bustle of the machine age. The technology in this poem is represented by the train. Trains run along tracks in set directions; you can't  do a U-turn very easily in a train, I expect. And Thomas' train is an 'express', a crucial detail only added in the final draft of the poem. So, this train is going swiftly, inexorably in one direction, into the future.

It stops, however, 'unwontedly'. This is an interesting and significant adverb. Firstly, it sounds rather archaic, an older word from a different time to the modern 'express-train'. Secondly it tells us that the stop at Adlestrop was unintended, unexpected and unscheduled. So the poet hasn't chosen consciously to pause on his onward journey; the pause has happened by chance. Thirdly, though it has a different meaning, when we hear 'unwontedly' we surely also hear the more common 'unwantedly'. If you were delayed on your journey to work/ school for no apparent reason wouldn't you find this irritating and unwanted? Though we know deep down that we all need to relax, sometimes we can be reluctant and resistant to taking time-out to de-stress, even though we know contact with the natural world is a powerful stress-buster.

But this train stops. And an unexpected, unbidden moment of ruminative quietness opens up for the poet. And into this space-in-time flows an appreciation of simple, natural beauty, almost a Wordsworthian communion with nature that lifts the spirits and stirs the soul. Most readers, surely, can identify with these feelings and this experience.

Nebulous intangible beauty

There's something about the easy-seeming, unforced way *Adlestrop* is written that adds to its power. As we've said, Thomas made a career as a writer of prose – reviews, articles and other such journalistic work – before the poet Robert Frost suggested he could turn his fine prose into finer poetry. As with other of his poems, Thomas wrote prose notes about the experience captured in this poem and then concentrated them into verse. And, though the poem has a loose tetrameter, a cross rhyme scheme and some internal rhymes, it retains some of the pliancy of prose. Take the first line, for instance. It starts with a simple affirmative, as if in answer to a question, posed by another character or the speaker himself. The following lines are unhurried and contemplative, their syntax expressing the cadences of speech. It would have been more efficient to write:

'I remember the name Adlestrop because one hot afternoon in June the express-train stopped there unwontedly.'

Pupils sometimes struggle to appreciate the distinct qualities of verse, so here's an opportunity to highlight these. What's been lost, if anything, by my neatening up, prosefying and streamlining of Thomas's lines?

A major loss is in terms of movement and rhythm. Rather boldly, and certainly significantly, Thomas' poem pauses after its first word, and at a single three-lettered syllable at that. Then there's another longer pause, indicated by the hyphen at the end of the first line, as if the speaker is thinking, remembering. Similarly, there's a pause, a caesura, after 'unwontedly', which both mimics the train's coming to a stop and allows the reader a moment to take on board the significance of a word moved deliberately into prime position at the start of a line. Suitably, the stanza ends with another full-stop. Making the reader halt for a moment after 'name' generates another slight pause when we hear the internal rhyme word, 'train'. Sonically 'drew' is superior to 'stopped' as it chimes gently with 'noon' and 'June', the latter of which Thomas places as the last word, concluding the stanza in gentle harmony.

Japanese garden's sometimes have water features from which single drops of water make a quiet plopping sound. The point of such features is not to draw attention to the sound of the water, but tune us to the deep silence around it. Thomas uses quiet sounds in a similar way to create a hush of attention:

'The steam hissed. Someone cleared his throat.'

A moment stops, holds and stretches; a space defined by what is not happening, 'no one left and no one came', by its quietness and by absence and emptiness – the platform is 'bare'. The poet prolongs the same of stillness and stasis by repeating the same phrase about Adlestrop at the end of the second stanza and by once again adding a hyphen, as if time is stuck in closed loop. He develops the static, entranced effect by emptying the third stanza of verbs. And into the contemplative, restful silence comes the sound of a blackbird's song.

The poet wouldn't have seen the English flora he appreciatively lists, nor would he have heard the bird's song if the train hadn't stopped and near silence descended. How often do we notice the natural beauty of birdsong as we busily go about our lives? Simple beauty. And blackbirds are particularly beloved by poets – more recently Wallace Stevens and Seamus Heaney have written poems about them. Perhaps, in part, poets identify themselves with songbirds and especially with the often overlooked, unexotic ones such as the fairly common-or-garden blackbird. To me, it seems that Thomas, a solitary man by all accounts, appreciates and identifies with both the remote and 'lonely fair' [ness] of the clouds and with the solitary bird singing. Moreover, around this single blackbird, 'round him', as if in support, is a choir composed of 'all the birds', an image of community and mutual harmony. And, of course, Thomas expresses this nebulous beauty beautifully. In particular the synaesthetic transformation of sound into sight - birdsong sounding 'mistier' - is a masterstroke. In addition, the poem ends with a sense of the poet's consciousness opening up and moving outwards, widening, expanding from that single song, tuning and almost dissolving into a deeper, profoundly English music.

Adlestrop distilled:

REMEMBER – NAME – EXPRESS-TRAIN – UNWONTEDLY – HISSED – NO – BARE – ADLESTROP – WILLOWS – MEADOWSWEET – LONELY – HIGH – BLACKBIRD – CLOSE – ALL – GLOUCESTERSHIRE.

 If you've got a very creative class, or you're very ambitious and like a challenge, you could start studying this poem by reading Thomas' diary notes and then ask your students to try to turn these into a poem; a useful and illuminating exercise that follows Thomas' own creative processes:

Then we stopped at Adlestrop, thro the willows cd be heard a chain of blackbirds songs at 12.45 & one thrush & no man seen, only a hiss of engine letting off steam. Stopping outside Campden by banks of long grass willow herb & meadowsweet, extraordinary silence between the two periods of travel . . . one man clears his throat - and a greater rustic silence. No house in view[.] Stop only for a minute till signal is up.

Robert Browning, *Home Thoughts from Abroad*

This other Eden

What does England and Englishness mean for us today in the age of Brexit? What are the key traits, if any, of English national character? How are the English distinct from the Welsh, Scottish or Irish? What are the key points in English history? Who are the greatest ever English men and women? What are

 the essential components of English culture? What is a quintessential English landscape? As the class come into your room have the national anthem playing very quietly in the background. Working individually pupils should write down the first twenty words or phrases that spring to mind when they

think of England and or Englishness. If they need a few prompts you could suggest: food items, such as roast dinner, fish and chips, a cup of tea; writers, such as Shakespeare, Dickens, Austen; icons and institutions such as the Houses of Parliament, Nelson's column, The Angel of the North, the BBC, Last Night of the Proms; significant historical figures, such as the two Queen Elizabeths, Margaret Thatcher, Winston Churchill, Walter Tull; legendary figures, such as King Arthur, Robin Hood, Boudica...

Only give the class a few teacher minutes – they should not overthink, just write whatever comes to mind. Next, they could compare their list with the pupil next to them and produce a combined list. Feedback in whole class discussion to produce an overall list. If you're feeling ambitious, try to rank the items 1-20. Obviously, there are competing ideas of Englishness, including a range of political readings that take patriotism into the more dangerous waters of nationalism. So, this is a topic that needs sensitive handling and respect must be shown to different opinions. Before examining the poem, ask pupils to conclude this introduction by writing a few lines about how  they feel to be English, British or whatever nationality they identify with. What are the best things about living in England? What are the worst? Do they feel proud to be English, indifferent about it, even ashamed? If they don't identify themselves with any particular nationality, but rather by gender, age, religion, race etc., ask them to reflect on why this might be. Return to this topic at the end of the lesson.

Approving speech

HTfB is a surprisingly sweet, sentimental poem for a poet probably now best known for intense dramatic monologues, such as *My Last Duchess, The Laboratory* and *Porphyria's Lover* written in the voices of disturbed and often murderous characters. It's surprising too in terms of the sentiment expressed – a wistful longing to be in England in order to appreciate the fauna and flora of an English spring. This is surprising because Browning had eloped from England to Italy in order to marry his wife, the poet Elizabeth Barrett Browning. After a marriage Elizabeth's family had expressly forbidden, the newly-weds did not rush back to the mother country, but continued instead to live, happily enough by all accounts, in the sunnier climes of the continent. As one critic remarked, somewhat tartly, Browning expresses a nostalgia for England, but not one strong enough to actually make him want to go there, other than, that is, in verse.

And this is very much an England of the mind, or the imagination - a timeless, pastoral vision of England that workers in the mills of the industrial revolution during the mid-nineteenth century might not have recognised as describing their world. Not that the characters in Browning's poem appreciate the natural beauty surrounding them. Though 'whoever' is in England 'sees' they do so 'unaware'. Hence the poet suggests that often we stop appreciating what is immediately around us. Only when we have  moved away from and have a more distant or different perspective can we see our immediate world again more fully. Perhaps this is why it could be easier for non-English people to define Englishness – it's hard to see ourselves from the inside. Browning certainly assumes that he needs to inform and educate the reader about what they have been missing about England. For example, he uses an imperative, 'Hark', to draw our unfocused attention, takes on a teacherly tone – 'that's the wise thrush' – and a comforting, vicarish manner – 'though' things may look 'rough', 'all will be gay when noontide wakes anew'.

Rose-tinted rapture!

Browning's celebration of England focuses on various aspects of nature, particularly trees, flowers, the rural landscape and song birds. For the poet, England is synonymous with a benign, fertile and gentle rural landscape, rather than say with its culture or cities or history or national character: Elms, apple and pear trees; blossom, clover, buttercups; orchard, hedge, fields; chaffinch, whitethroat, swallows, thrush. The rich variety of English nature also operates in perfect, peaceful harmony, as the poet exclaims in a consistently excited tone [note the preponderance of exclamation marks!]. Benevolently and bountifully, the personified 'pear-tree', for example, 'scatters' 'blossoms and dewdrops' like the fruits of its labour; the 'wise thrush' sings with carefree 'rapture', as if in ecstatic praise of an English summer; even the 'rough' looking 'fields' will be 'gay'; like a mother, the 'noontide wakes' from sleep the little buttercups which

72

are themselves nature's 'dower' for little children. There's no sense here of nature 'red in tooth and claw' or 'survival of the fittest', though Charles Darwin's *Origin of the Species* would be published only a few years later in 1859 and radically change Victorian understanding of the natural world. Nor is there a sense of a county that had recently declared war in the Crimea.

Browning's sonorous rhyming adds to the general sense of universal [though English] peacefulness, bounty and well-being. Generally he uses couplets and employs full rhyme sounds. In the final couplet, the poet makes a pointed comparison between English and foreign, presumably Italian, fauna. Not only are buttercups bright, they are 'far brighter than', hence aesthetically superior to the foreign 'melon-flower' whose brightness is cheap, vulgar and showy. Clearly the buttercup is being used here emblematically to suggest that England is brighter and more becomingly modest in its demeanour than 'gaudy' foreign climes.

Oh, to be in England

Return to the activities from the start of the lesson, but now bring Browning's poem into the discussion. How do pupils feel about England? Do they see themselves as English? Do they define their identities by nationality, or is identity a more composite idea constructed through multiple facets? Do they recognise Browning's vision of England as being about somewhere they live? Does the poem seem realistic or like an idealised version? Perhaps the poem is less about England and more about how we can romanticise things when we look back on them nostalgically.

Home Thoughts from Abroad crunched:

ENGLAND – WHOEVER – BOUGHS – LEAF – CHAFFINCH – NOW – MAY – SWALLOWS – HARK – SCATTERS – DEWDROPS – WISE – YOU – RAPTURE – ROUGH – GAY – BUTTERCUPS – BRIGHTER.

U.A. Fanthorpe, *First Flight*

Give me five

The poet and academic Simon Armitage recommends an incisive method for engaging with any poem. Armitage suggests that readers start by identifying five interesting words and work outwards from these to a wider consideration. So, let's try to apply the Armitage method to Fanthorpe's gently humorous, wryly comic duologue which contrasts two characters' responses to flying.

Which words would you select for closer inspection? Before continuing to read this essay, write down what you consider to be the most important or most interesting words in the poem. For me, the first word that sticks out is the verb 'slithers'. Normally 'slithers' is used to describe the unnerving, zig-zagging movements of snakes as they cross ground. Here the poet tells us that the earth 'slithers' and this word works in several ways. Firstly, it suggests speedy, winding movement. Secondly, the surprisingness of the word for the reader replicates the surprising sensation the speaker feels as the plane took off. And thirdly the connotations of snakes come into play. For many people snakes are frightening, potentially dangerous creatures. Seeing a snake slithering sends alarm signals to most people's brains. At a push we might even bring the evil connotations of snakes into the equation, connotations forged by their unfortunate role in the story of Adam and Eve and man's fall.

The other words I'd select are two adjectives, 'familiar' and 'nimble', an abstract noun, 'History' and a common noun, 'wigs'. Granted, 'familiar' is not a particularly interesting word in and of itself. It's the sort of abstract and colourless word that some poets would strenuously avoid. We don't hear or see or touch or smell the word 'familiar'. Nor does Fanthorpe use the adjective in an unusual way, such as grammatically engineering it into a different function or by combining it unexpectedly with other words, as in 'the familiar tarantula in your bowl of cornflakes'. Nevertheless, it's important in this poem because the whole thing is about leaving behind what the poet is fondly used to and embracing new experience.

Like all art, and poetry, in particular, flight is a defamiliarising experience, changing our perspective and the way we see the world. An example of this is my third choice, the adjective 'nimble'. Normally we'd use this word to describe how someone or something moves athletically – zippily, agilely, deftly. Nimble things also tend to be small; hence the football commentators' phrase 'quite nimble for a big guy'. Being substantial and static, or at least slow moving to the naked eye, normally the sun would not be described through personification as 'nimble'. Up in the skies, however, the world seems to operate differently. The fixed points we normally navigate ourselves around are suddenly in motion or seem to be. Like us, up in the air, the world seems to become unfixed.

I've picked the word 'history' because it seems at odds with the words that precede and surround it. Up until this point in the poem the main speaker has focused on describing their sensory experience and their feelings about flying: The odd, disconcerting movement; the fear of leaving the familiar; the play of light; the soft colour and texture of the clouds ['meringue' might have made it into this discussion if Mr. Armitage had allowed us six words]. 'History' signals a change in tone, perspective and to the scale of the speaker's observations. Now they are thinking more profoundly, reflectively and philosophically, pondering the significance of being disconnected from the earth, up in the clouds, seemingly beyond the reach of the past and even of time.

In my judgement, 'wigs' is a surprising word in this context. Unlike her use of 'familiar', in this case, Fanthorpe also combines a surprising word in a surprising way. What exactly are '*mackerel* wigs'? Presumably they are not wigs worn by mackerels, as mackerels are a type of fish and no type of fish I know of is likely to be found sporting any sort of wig, in any context – for one thing how would they put them on? Perhaps 'mackerel wigs' are something in themselves, maybe the phrase is idiomatic, and I just haven't heard of it. Put that idea to trial, google it, and absolutely nothing comes up. As far as google is 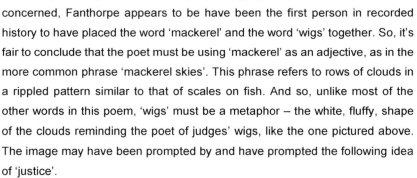 concerned, Fanthorpe appears to be have been the first person in recorded history to have placed the word 'mackerel' and the word 'wigs' together. So, it's fair to conclude that the poet must be using 'mackerel' as an adjective, as in the more common phrase 'mackerel skies'. This phrase refers to rows of clouds in a rippled pattern similar to that of scales on fish. And so, unlike most of the other words in this poem, 'wigs' must be a metaphor – the white, fluffy, shape of the clouds reminding the poet of judges' wigs, like the one pictured above. The image may have been prompted by and have prompted the following idea of 'justice'.

Beyond single words

So, how useful has the Armitage method been? Certainly it's incisive and focuses attention on specific aspects of diction, a fundamental aspect of any poem. But what are its weaknesses? For one thing, words tend to come in groups and are affected by their immediate context. Syntax is not merely decorative – in English it often shapes meaning [compare 'the man ate the sausages' to 'the sausages ate the man']. I slightly deviated from the Armitage method in the final example because, surely, it's the combination 'mackerel wigs' that's more interesting than either individual word. In fact, the whole line is interesting and odd – with clouds that look like disembodied, fish-scaled wigs 'dispensing' the 'justice of air', whatever that might be. Perhaps being so high up has made the poet rather giddily fanciful. Similarly, although 'history' is incongruous in the context, surely it's qualified significantly by the preceding words, 'we have come too high for', which suggest the speaker feels detached both from the earth and the past.

Moreover, the comic element of the poem is generated by the contrasts between the two speakers and the relationship between their lines. At first, while the first speaker is feeling nervous and ill-at-ease on their first flight, the second speaker, a relative veteran of flying, sounds perfectly blasé: 'This is a short hop for me'. Their speech also cuts through the middle of the first speaker's sentence, as if interrupting them rudely mid-flow. As these interruptions continue it seems the second speaker is not really listening to or responding at all to what the first speaker says. This is not a conversation, but more like two interlocking, but independent monologues. In fact, it seems, at times that both speakers are deliberately ignoring what the other says. Moreover, as the poem goes on the second speaker starts saying more, but this has absolutely no impact on the first. For example, the response to their question about suitable attire, 'know what I mean?' is not graced with any answer at all, or, indeed, even any acknowledgement that they've spoken or, indeed, exist. And even when they use an imperative, 'Go on, say it', they're disregarded.

Adding to the comic effect, the more poetic the first speaker gets, the more prosaic and matter-of-fact the second becomes. As one goes up in style, the other goes down. In other words, there's a rich comic contrast in their tones and the language they use. Speaker one is emotive, poetic and lyrical. She uses delicate metaphors and, in painterly fashion, describes what she can see – the 'meringue kingdom' of the clouds; the 'crinkled tangerine' of the light. As we've noted, she philosophises, ponders, even uses a clever paradox in the final line that also wittily alludes to the story of Icarus. In starkest contrast, speaker two speaks of purely practical matters and in an ordinary, everyday idiom. There's a witty irony here – speaker one, uneasy at actually being in the air, takes flight in her imagination and language, while speaker two, comfortable physically off the ground, retains a decidedly grounded, down-to-earth manner of speaking. Tellingly, in terms of the relationship, it is the first speaker, perhaps the poet herself, who has both the first and last words and the most memorable ones.

Adcock's entertaining poem dramatises the fear of leaving a familiar place and becoming disconnected from it, in this case the place is England. But this England isn't the green and pleasant land of other poems in this cluster, such as Browning's or Thomas'; Fanthorpe will miss England's ordinary, unromantic features, its 'motorways, reservoir' and its 'building sites'. In other words, it's not beauty she will miss, but just the ordinary, comfortingly familiar, everyday world.

First Flight shrunk:

LIKE – SUSPECT – SLITHERS – ANGLE – ME – READ – DEAR – JUST – FAMILIAR – NIMBLE – US – VANISHES – MERINGUE – MED – TANGERINE – HOME – OVERCOAT – NEED – PULLOVER – HISTORY – TOMORROW – CONFOUNDS – KNOW – YOU'D – WRONG – SAY – WIGS – TOO.

Fleur Adcock, *Stewart Island*

~~Mad seagulls~~

Google 'Stewart Island, New Zealand' and the first website that comes up is a promotional page for tourists which highlights the island's various attractions:

'To all our visitors our Island offers a special experience - a glimpse into a simpler, slower lifestyle, in rhythm with the sea and the tides, attuned to the natural world of bush and beach...Whether you have come to enjoy the land and seascapes, view the wildlife, walk, boat, fish, dive, kayak, hunt or just relax, a Stewart Island holiday will be an experience that will draw you back here again and again.'

Scroll through the rest of the website's pages and you'll find plenty that make the island appear a lovely holiday destination. Even in black and white, the picture of the landscape at the top of the previous page looks inviting, doesn't it, with its sandy beach, gentle, possibly warm sea, abundant flora and absence of people – a popular combination of attributes for tourism. No mention here of maliciously crazed and aggressive sea birds, too-cold-to-swim-in water or horrible biting insects.

Stewart Island is also called Rakiura, from the Maori, often translated as 'glowing skies', which also makes it sound attractive. A smallish island, with only 300 or so people living on it, it offers tourists peace and quiet and solitude. What's not to like? A fair amount, it seems, according to this small, short prosaic poem that looks like an island of words on the blank whiteness of the page. And a key issue, the poem, suggests is that there is a huge difference between places that are attractive to visit and ones where we may want to actually live.

Too cold to swim

What's the difference between prose and poetry? Clearly in a prose poem there's not much difference, but Adcock's isn't a prose poem. Arguably poetry is a more intense, more concentrated form than prose. Unarguably a distinguishing characteristic is how poems are set out on the page, their form and lineation. *Stewart Island* is written in the down-to-earth, conversational style that Adcock often employs. Characteristically the poet eschews fancy poetic devices and avoids any extravagant flourishes. The language is plain and direct, like ordinary, everyday speech[3] [so much so that Adcock can drop direct speech into the poem without it seeming out of place and write lines with apparently clumsy close repetitions, such as 'live there. True there was...'] and the tone is matter-of-fact. Moreover, there are no complex or unusual words and the language is also used literally – there's no extravagant figurative imagery. So, stylistically the poem reads a lot like prose and is very accessible to readers. What then, if anything, is achieved by the way Adcock

---

[3] Adcock has said that 'The tone' she feels 'at home in is one in which' she 'can address people without embarrassing them' and that she would like readers 'to relax and listen as if to an intimate conversation'.

has arranged the words on the page? To what extent is this poem just prose arranged typographically to look like poetry? To foreground this question you could first present the poem in prose form and challenge the class to re-arrange it as a poem. They'll need to think of where lines break and run on, about caesuras and stanza form. Hence, here's the poem proseiated:

'But look at all this beauty,' said the hotel manager's wife when asked how she could bear to live there. True: there was a fine bay, all hills and atmosphere; white sand, and bush down to the sea's edge; oyster-boats, too, and Maori fishermen with Scottish names (she ran off with one that autumn). As for me, I walked on the beach; it was too cold to swim. My seven-year-old collected shells and was bitten by sand-flies; my four-year-old paddled, until a mad seagull jetted down to jab its claws and beak into his head. I had already decided to leave the country.

Frankly, it's hard to see that very much has been achieved by the poetic form. Perhaps using only one, complete, unbroken stanza is effective. As well as visually suggesting a thin island of words, the form implies both solitariness and a robust singularity of view. There's no gap in this solid block of text for another viewpoint to be properly expressed, nor space for the speaker to change their mind. In terms of lineation, both enjambment and caesura are used a few times at points where Adcock stops a line to create a significant pause, as in after 'until' and 'shells'. Some lines are arranged to sound more stark and emphatic than they would if they were presented as prose, notably the final one.

There's no metre, so the lines fall rather flatly. No euphony is orchestrated through the harmonising sonic effect of rhyme. Is there, in fact, any principle governing the shape and length of the poem's lines? Yes, the poem is arranged as syllabic verse. Count the syllables and you'll discover a pattern of alternating lines of seven and eight syllables. So what? Well, this creates an underpinning structure to hold the poem together and give it shape, and the alternating pattern subtly encodes a sense of alternative arrangements, albeit alternatives that are only one syllable different.

No rose-tinted romanticism

The language of advertising and tourism accentuates and often exaggerates the positives while ignoring any negatives. In stark contrast, stripped back and matter-of-fact, Adcock's language tells things straight. The poem starts in media res, mid-conversation, with the hotel manager's wife answering an implied question. Initially the poet's description matches the tourist boards with a list of the island's attractive features – a 'fine bay', 'hills', 'white sand' and abundant fauna. However, unlike the tourist board, the poet has already signalled her negative feelings about this place. She has asked the wife how she could 'bear' to 'live there'. The verb seems excessive, as if must take rare endurance or stupidity to put with all this natural beauty, and 'there' rather than 'here' already indicates the poet's sense of separation from the landscape. On the other hand, Adcock accepts that there is beauty and acknowledges some intriguing local cultural hybridity – 'Maori fishermen with Scottish names'. But she also undercuts the manager's wife's praise [in an entertainingly pointed aside] and goes on to undermine each seemingly attractive feature of the island. The water at the beach is 'too cold to swim in'; one child is 'bitten by sand flies' while another is attacked by a mad seagull, somewhat hyperbolically described as having 'jetted' down to viciously 'jab is claws and beak'. Indeed, it seems that this landscape is actively hostile to the poet as well as to her kin.

Tense, brief, anecdotal, prosaic, unromantic, this poem ends with a simple declarative statement and an emphatic full stop. According to the New Zealand Book Council, 'Although Adcock's range is wide, her oeuvre like her life, she has said, is 'influenced, infected, and to some sense distorted' by questions of national identity. Many poems are written from the perspective of an ambivalent outsider; identifying with and yet withdrawing from various emotional and physical contexts.'[4] Adcock started her life in New Zealand but moved to England as a child and remained here. I'm not sure that she's very ambivalent in this poem about Stewart Island, which incidentally, seems to function as a microcosm for the whole country of New Zealand. Whilst the poet does acknowledge some attractive features, only a cretin, or an Australian perhaps,

---

[4] http://www.bookcouncil.org.nz/writer/adcock-fleur/

would employ her to write advertising copy for the New Zealand tourism board.

Sometimes places can make us want to stay in them. We may feel we belong in a particular place, at home there. Other people may want to escape from seemingly boring environs to places more dynamic and glamorous, or from busy big city life to the quieter charms of the countryside. Small town life can seem parochial and claustrophobic to some people, especially when we're growing up and life can seem to be going on in more interesting ways elsewhere, in bigger places with wider horizons. Adcock's poem successfully conveys a negative response to a small place that might well seem a beautiful idyll to an outsider.

Stewart Island crushed:

BEAUTY – HOTEL – BEAR – TRUE – ATMOSPHERE – SAND – MAORI – SCOTTISH – RAN OFF – ME – COLD – SEVEN-YEAR-OLD – BITTEN – PADDLED – MAD – CLAWS – ALREADY – LEAVE.

Moniza Alvi, *Presents from my Aunts in Pakistan*

Neither here nor there

Sometimes it is best to enter a big room through a small door, or so a wise woman once told me, rather enigmatically. The small door I'm going to use to enter Alvi's vibrant poem is the last four lines:

'And I was there -
of no fixed nationality,
Staring through fretwork
At the Salimar Gardens.'

In many ways, thematically, stylistically and formally these concluding lines summarise the poem that precedes them. Firstly, we have the first-person voice, telling us about a personal experience. Secondly, the importance of place is emphasised by the word 'there' and that this is an 'other' place for the speaker, not a 'here' where they feel at home. The next lines summarises the poem's central theme - the struggle the speaker has in reconciling her hybrid identity, a struggle that leaves her feeling disconnected and unfixed in a liminal,

84

in-between space. Fourthly, her sense of separation from, but also fascination with, Pakistan, the country of her forefathers, and therefore tied up with ideas of origins, is signalled by the verb 'staring'. The poet is not participating in the culture, but instead looks at with fixed intensity. Except that, as the second half of that line tell us, she is not looking directly at the object of her interest. Instead she is looking 'through fretwork'. Fretwork can be highly ornate with few gaps, so the image suggests that the poet's view is partial, obscured, fragmentary - she hasn't a clear view and cannot see the complete picture. Seventhly, she's staring at the 'Shalimar Gardens' which is a park in Lahore, Pakistan. To English readers this is an exotic, unfamiliar, 'other' place and even the sound of the word 'shalimar' carries a whiff of magic. But these gardens are a very popular tourist destination, so even when Alvi is looking at Pakistan she is only looking at what outsiders, tourists, see. Like the exotic and European clothes referred to throughout the poem, 'Shalimar gardens' works as a metonym, a part standing in for a whole. Here the metonym stands in for Pakistan and Pakistani culture as a whole.

Shapeshifting, side-winding form

And there's more to the lines than the words. We might note that the lines are all rather short, that they don't begin as they would do conventionally in poetry – i.e. with capital letters, and that there's no metre or rhyme scheme to lend them a predictable shape or pattern. But more significant, of course, is the way Alvi lays them out, typographically, on the page. In the original the lines start at different places on the page:

> and I was there -
>   of no fixed nationality,
>   staring through fretwork
>   At the Shalimar Gardens.

Clearly this pattern encodes movement and uncertainty into the poem; it is the formal manifestation of the speaker's sense of unfixedness.

If you're a teacher, to emphasise this point, perhaps the first time you present the poem, or maybe better just the first stanza, to the class arrange the lines in a standardised form so that they all start at least in the same place:

'They sent me a salwar kameez
Peacock-blue,
And another,
Glistening like an orange split open,
Embossed slippers, gold and black
Points curling' [and so forth]

Even in this more regular arrangement there's a lot of unpredictability: With no obvious principle governing the length of lines, they vary from two words to eight and from three syllables, at the shortest, to ten at the longest. Where the lines end is unpredictable, but also, in Alvi's more protean form, where lines begin is also unpredictable. And this is a poem about uncertain starts [or origins/ beginnings and the poet's 'birthplace'] and unpredictable ends [or outcomes]. Another method for emphasising the significance of the lineation in *Presents from my Aunts in Pakistan* would be to give the class the shape of the poem without the individuals words and ask them to make intelligent surmises about the possible content. Something like this:

....
        ....,
        ....
....,
....
      ....
....
      ....
....
    .... -
....

If you're feeling ambitious, you could even give half the class the words stripped of the shifting, snaking form and the other half the form without the words. After a few teacher minutes, pupils from each half of the class could then be paired and bring their insights together. They could then read the rest of the poem.

In some ways the form of the poem is unpredictable and irregular but in other ways it is predictable. An example of the former is how the length of stanzas vary, fifteen lines followed by eleven, then seven and so forth. Certainly, Alvi is not employing a consistent stanza form, nor one that is a recognisable conventional one, such as a quatrain. On the other hand, each long, winding stanza ends with a full stop and within each stanza the lines follow a similar unsettled and unfixed pattern. Again, this tension embodies the poem's central concerns - the feeling of being caught in-between Pakistani and English identities.

Glistening like an orange split open

What else is striking about Alvi's poem? Firstly, it's full of visual imagery and bright, bold colours dominate the opening: 'Peacock-blue'; 'orange'; 'gold and black'; 'candy-striped'; 'apple-green'; 'silver-bordered'. Later there's also reference to fire, 'stained glass' and more 'gold'. Secondly, the description of these clothes conveys the ambivalence the poet felt as a child. In this sense the clothes work, like the Gardens, as a metonym for Pakistani life and culture. On the positive side, the clothes look bright, they are 'radiant' and inviting, almost edible – 'like an orange'; 'candy-coloured'; 'apple-green'. They are also associated with precious metals, particularly gold and silver. But on the negative side, the bangles cause pain, they 'snapped, drew blood'. Trying such strikingly, lovely, flamboyant clothes on also made the poet feel 'alien', dressed up like an actor in a 'costume', leaving her longing for familiar western clothes, 'denim and corduroy'. Tactile imagery further underlines her discomfort and self-consciousness: 'My costume clung to me'. Worse, she feels embarrassed, maybe even in pain again, 'I was aflame'. Later in the poem she is afflicted by 'prickly heat' and thinks of Pakistan as a 'throbbing' land. The symbolic 'camel-skin lamp' works in a similar way. On the one hand, it is beautiful and entrancing, throwing colours 'like stained glass', making the poet 'marvel'. But on the other hand, the creation of the lamp has involved 'cruelty'.

Alvi ends the poem describing Pakistan as a 'fractured land', throbbing powerfully, like a heart. And she too is fractured. Or rather she *felt* fractured. Unlike her Aunt Jamilia, she was unable to make herself 'half-English' and half-Pakistani. She tried to understand herself, get a grip on her shifting sense of identity, tried to 'glimpse' herself in the 'mirror-work' of the clothes and by recalling her past, her story of origins. She finishes saying she felt she had 'no fixed nationality'. But, the poem is set in the past, when the poet was a child or teenager; 'I *was* there'. All of us, as teenagers, struggle to some extent with the process of becoming adults and of forging our individual sense of self. As an adult and as a poet, Alvi knows her upbringing means she can draw on two rich and enriching cultures, a creative hybridity that surely helped to write a poem bold enough to find its own, unconventional form and use aspects of Pakistani culture, such as the 'salmar kameez', a 'sari', the 'camel-skin lamp', Lahore and the 'Shalimar Gardens' and helped her to express herself eloquently in the English language.

[As this is a longish poem, I'm not going to pick a word from every line.]

Presents from my Aunts in Pakistan shrunk:

SALWAR – PEACOCK – GLISTENING – GOLD – CANDY-STRIPED – BLOOD – LIKE – PAKISTAN – WERE – SARI – SILVER-BORDERED – TEENS – SATIN-SILKEN – ALIEN – NEVER - LONGED – DENIM – COSTUME – AFLAME –

COULDN'T – HALF-ENGLISH – CAMEL-SKIN – CRUELTY – MARVEL – MOTHER – INDIAN – STOLEN – RADIANT – CARDIGANS – IMPRESS – WEEKEND – MIRROR-WORK – MYSELF – GLASS – ENGLAND – SCREAMING – COT – ENGLISH – BIRTHPLACE – FRACTURED – THROBBING – LAHORE – AUNTS – SCREENED – PRESENTS – BEGGARS – THERE – NATIONALITY – FRETWORK – SHALIMAR.

Grace Nichols, *Hurricane Hits England*

Born in 1950 in Guyana, a South American country that is part of the Caribbean, Grace Nichols moved permanently to live in England in 1977. Gently infused with a Caribbean voice and sensibility, Nichols' rhythmically rich poetry often explores issues of culture, identity and immigration.

Blinding illuminations

The key concept and technique in Nichols' poem is mixing or, to use a fancier term, hybridity. Like Guyana's dual South American and Caribbean culture, many aspects of the poem are an alloy of two different elements. Take, for instance, the title, which combines an extreme feature of violent tropical weather with England. As you'll probably be aware, we don't normally have hurricanes in England. Ordinarily, we're much more likely to have far less dramatic weather, such as grey skies and persistent drizzle. Or take the poem's diction and phrasing. Some of the lines in Nichols' poem are written in an elevated form of Standard English [SE]; the first stanza, for instance. There is an obvious shift, however, in the second stanza, with the listing of exotic names for storm deities that themselves are a mixture of African and Mayan as well as male and female entities. A subtler example of the Caribbean influence on some of the poem's phrasing is the line 'tell me why you visit' which in SE would include an auxiliary verb and the present participle; 'tell me why you are visiting'. The perspective is also mixed. At the start of the poem Nichols is writing from a third-person point of view, observing a character – 'she lay awake' – and the poem's told retrospectively, in the past tense. However, third-person has merged seamlessly into first-person by the last line of the second stanza; '*My sweeping, back-home cousin*'. The poem is also composed of commands that empower the speaker and questions that convey her uncertainty. For example, the series of imperatives in stanza two are balanced by the sequence of five questions in the succeeding stanzas. And, in turn, despite the 'sweet mystery', those questions are answered by the speaker in the final stanza where she explains the function and purpose of the storm, 'come to break...' and 'come to let...' Moreover, from the start the hurricane itself is presented ambivalently.

Simultaneously the storm is both 'fearful' and 'reassuring', which seems like a contradiction. At first this contradiction may seem impossible to resolve. How can we be afraid of something we also find 'reassuring'? On closer inspection, however, the apparent contradiction can be untangled. The storm is frightening because of its potential destructive power, its 'reaping' of 'havoc'. Personified to have its own will, its violence is also escalating ominously - 'gathering rage'. Moreover, it is 'dark' and therefore potentially threatening, perhaps even evil, and it is compared metaphorically to a disturbing ghost from the past - 'an ancestral spectre' - the return of something long buried now haunting the present. But, on the other hand, the storm is reassuring because it is familiar; it is 'ancestral', part of the speaker's cultural heritage. And the storm reveals the fundamental continuity between seemingly  disparate places, the Caribbean and England. Moreover, the destruction that it may cause can itself be positive; stirring, shaking and loosening things up, the hurricane breaks the metaphorical 'frozen lake' in the inner landscape of the poet's mind, and also releases the poet's locked-up feelings: 'O why is my heart unchained'. The sense of excited release here is emphasised both by the use of the emotive apostrophe and the unchaining of a single line from those either side of it.

The poem's fourth stanza contains the most powerful expression of the seemingly paradoxical power of the hurricane. It begins with an oxymoron, 'blinding illumination' and this apparent paradox is further developed through the bringing of light ['illumination'] as a consequence of loss of light - the storm 'short-circuits' the speaker into 'darkness'. The poem dramatises the unsettling, topsy-turvy effect of the storm on the speaker, the unleashing of an inner storm that builds towards a crisis. And then radical confusion gives suddenly way to dramatic revelation: The hurricane's message strikes the poet in a final line that ends with an emphatic, conclusive, storm-ending full-stop.

Stormy form

The form of the poem is irregular but could have been even more so. What difference would it make, for instance, if the poem was arranged as if the words have been blown apart by the hurricane? Something like this:

It took a hurricane,   to bring her   closer

To the landscape
     Half the night   she lay   awake,

  The howling ship of the wind,

                 Its gathering rage,

     Like some   dark   ancestral   spectre.

Fearful and
      reassuring.

  Talk to me Hurracan
     Talk to me Oya
Talk to me Shango

       And Hattie

In Nichols' arrangement the poem's structure is able to withstand the violent disruptive force of the storm. Nevertheless, her building made of words is battered about a bit, particularly in the opening stanzas. On the one hand, each line starts in the same place and with a capital letter and each line is embedded within a solid, protective stanzaic block. Each of these stanzas is also self-contained, ending in alignment with their last sentence, as signalled by the punctuation. In these ways the words look fairly robust. No single stray word or phrase is isolated from their block of text. And the first stanzas are roughly of the same shape and size with 7, 5 and 6 lines respectively. On the other hand,

 these stanzas are irregular, with different lengths and the lengths of lines are also erratic, as a glance down the ragged right-hand side of the poem confirms. In addition, the poem has no governing metre or shaping rhyme scheme to preserve order. Many of its lines are very short, as if winnowed by the wind, but they grow longer and more solid as the poem unfolds. Both the line lengths and stanzas become more regular by the fourth stanza, as if things are settling down and the crisis point has been passed. In short, the poem, like the landscape and the poet, may suffer and be shaped by the violence of the weather, but is also shown to survive and to endure.

The howling ship

What else makes the poem powerful and memorable? Perhaps the sense of the speaker in intense, urgent communication with the wild spirit of the storm. Certainly, the poem's rhythmic charge and its rich figurative imagery.

The verse's rhythmic pulse generates a building sense of excitement, working towards the dramatic lightning bolt revelation of a universal truth. The key engine driving rhythm is the rhetorical device of repetition. Phrases such as 'Talk to me' are repeated in quick succession, in this case three times. There are five consecutive questions, two of which begin with 'what is the meaning of?'. 'I am [+ present tense participle]' and 'come to' are repeated three times; 'mystery' [twice] and, of course, then there is final line:

'The earth is the earth is the earth'

The imagery is another important aspect. For me the most striking metaphorical images in the poem are the following:

- The howling ship of the wind
- Trees/ Falling heavy as wales
- The frozen lake in me
- Shaking the foundations of the very trees within me.

Is there anything that surprises you about the first of these images? Well, you might notice that ships don't tend to 'howl'. A howling wind is a conventional image, so what does 'ship' add? Clearly the poet wanted the sense of travel – the wind as a kind of ship in which the storm deities ride. The image also suggests a ship under terrible strain, almost being broken apart. Perhaps, coupled with the 'dark ancestral spectre', there is a subtle evocation of the horror of the slave ships that travelled from between Africa, Europe and the Caribbean with their human cargoes. Finally, the 'ship' image implies a radical confusion - a fundamental loss of distinction between land and water, as if the storm is so great, the rain so torrential that the land has become an ocean. This idea is re-enforced by the later image of trees being like 'wales'.

The second pair of images connect the outer landscape, battered by the storm to the speaker's inner mindscape. While the former is being transformed by the destructive power of the hurricane so too is the latter, but in a much more positive sense. The image of the 'frozen lake' suggests that the speaker has been living a shallow existence on the surface of herself, cut off from her own depths, just as she feels isolated until now

from the English landscape. These depths contain her personal history, her cultural heritage and her suppressed feelings. 'Frozen' obviously also suggests emotional coldness. By allowing herself to identify, 'align' with and 'follow' it, rather than resist its force, the hurricane becomes liberating for the speaker, breaking and shaking things up, forcing new formulations, reviving frozen feelings and bringing fresh new thought to the mind's attention. A fresh new thought that conveys a universal principle of our common humanity.

Hurricane Hits England crunched:

CLOSER – LANDSCAPE – AWAKE – SHIP – RAGE – SPECTRE – REASSURING – TALK – OYA – ME – HATTIE – BACK-HOME – WHY – ENGLISH – MEANING – TONGUES – HAVOC – NEW – ILLUMINATION – EVEN – US – DARKNESS – TREES – WALES – ROOTS – GRAVES – HEART – TROPICAL – ALIGNING – FOLLOWING – MYSTERY – SWEET – BREAK – SHAKING – KNOW – EARTH.

Tatamkhulu Afrika, *Nothing's Changed*

Long walk to freedom

In 1997, after spending twenty-seven years as a political prisoner, Nelson Mandela was released from Robben Island prison. A few years later Mandela led the African National Congress into South Africa's first ever democratic elections. Elected as South Africa's first ever black president, Mandela sped up the dismantling of the system of racial discrimination known as Apartheid. [Apartheid had operated at all levels and through all aspects of South African society, but by 1993 it was falling apart.] After decades of oppression, finally a cruelly racist and brutal system of government was being demolished and, miraculously, South Africa was making the painful transition to democracy without the chaos and bloodletting that many commentators had predicted.

As the great statesman put it in his autobiography, as he heard confirmation of his momentous election victory 'after more than three centuries, the white minority was conceding defeat and turning over power to the black majority'. Addressing the ANC that evening the newly elected, black president of South Africa added that, 'This is one of the most important moments in the life of our country. I stand here before you filled with deep pride and joy – pride in the ordinary, humble people of this country. You have shown such a calm, patient determination to reclaim this country as our own, and now the joy that we can loudly proclaim from the rooftops – Free at last! Free at last! I stand before you humbled by your courage, with a heart full of love for all of you. I regard it as the highest honour to lead the ANC at this moment in our history. I am your servant.... It is not the individuals that matter, but the collective...This is a time to heal the old wounds and build a new South Africa'.[5]

Then and now

This is a poem about contrasts; contrasts between the harsh landscape of District Six and the flash, up-market restaurant; between the restaurant and the working man's café nearby; between how the poet felt as a child and how he's made to feel now, and most crucially about the contrasting state of the country before and after the fall of Apartheid and white rule. Only the central point of the poem, as the title tells us frankly, is that despite the destruction of the Apartheid state and many of the race-bound injustices it perpetuated, returning to South Africa [the poem was written in 1994] the poet is angry to find that his country remains deeply and unjustly divided by class, wealth and most especially by race.

Read the first line of the poem aloud and you'll hear how those small, hard, separate monosyllables sound tough, hard and angry. The poet feels likes a small, hard, round stone in a landscape whose raggedness is reflected in the poem's stanza form. And he knows, instinctively, that he's in District Six, inner city Cape Town. Here, despite the friendly atmosphere suggested by the personified 'amiable weeds' the poet grows increasing angry, as conveyed by the repetitions of stanza two. Repetition and building up of syntax - 'and my'/ 'and the' etc., plus the intimate tactile imagery of skin and lungs, plus multiplying

---

[5] *Long Walk to Freedom*, pp. 611-612

adjectives, plus the increasing length of each line = tremendous escalation of tension. Of these adjectives 'inwards' is the most surprising, as it suggests some of the poet's anger is turned on himself, as if he is blaming himself.

Echoic effects, a simile and an ugly metaphor convey the poet's animosity towards the 'new, up-market' restaurant. The harsh, aggressive sound of 'brash' is emphasised by being echoed in 'glass', 'flag' and later 'grass' and by the verb 'flaring'. Alliteration enhances the impact of 'flaring like a flag', a simile

that suggests military conquest and the staking-out of territory. The verb 'squats' implies that the building is illegally occupying the space, that it is temporary and also links it to ugly animals, such as toads. The stanza ends more directly and bluntly: 'whites only inn' and with a bitter, sardonic tone; 'we know where we belong'. As with the instinctive understanding that the poet is in District Six, this line implies that years of conditioning/ brainwashing has led to citizens picking up and internalising culturally-coded signals about power, race and class. They don't have to consciously think about where they supposedly 'belong' according to authority, they know it automatically. That's how indoctrination works.

The restaurant interior is delicate; its restrained elegance contrasts with the outer brashness and with the rough, uncultivated landscape of 'grass and weeds' in which it sits. Once again the poet emphases that he's already familiar with this sort of exclusive swankiness. He doesn't have to look to know what sort of a place this is. The 'linen' and 'rose' are potent symbols and in a poem about race, the adjective 'white' takes on greater symbolic significance. Afrika juxtaposes the up-market place with a 'working man's café' that sells cheap curries ['bunny chows'], has only rudimentary furniture a ['plastic table's top'] and in which refined manners are not required and would be out of place. Again the poet uses bitter, dark irony, implying that the rudimentary roughness of the surroundings suits the black and working class population because their inferiority is innate, 'in the bone'. Again, the poet spits such racial and racist indoctrination back at his country, just as he will again, rhetorically, in the next stanza when he refers to his 'mean mouth'.

The visceral effect of being made to feel inferior, of being excluded on the basis of class and race from the supposedly 'finer' things of life and of this discrimination continuing to operate *still,* even after the fall of Apartheid and the election of Mandela and the ANC, makes the poet feel like time has turned back and no progress has been made. Nothing seems to have changed in South Africa; not just since the fall of Apartheid, but since the middle-aged poet was a child. And all that pent- up rage and burning frustration at this injustice pushes the poet to the verge of the sort of destructive violence many commentators had predicted would happen as South Africa tried to transform itself: 'Hands burn/ for a stone, a bomb'.

Nothing's Changed is a bitterly angry, blisteringly forthright poem. It's a cry of rage and protest against the seeming intractability of discrimination and injustice. Afrika uses the high-status cultural form of poetry to express his fierce

protest and as a form of eloquent testimony to the lie about his people being in any sense inferior to their white masters. It's also an unsentimental poem, resisting the temptation to present the new, black-governed South Africa in positive, propagandist terms. With its short, punchy lines, emphatic repetitions, potent symbolism and metaphor, the poem is like a piece of political rhetoric. It is a poem we could imagine being declaimed from a stage or a soapbox with a megaphone. This situation, the posh restaurant and the working-class café operate as metonyms – what happens here is emblematic of what is happening throughout South African society, the poem implies. It leaves the reader in no doubts about the strong feelings and strong convictions forcefully expressed. And, though the poem's clearly about a particular time and a particular place, its message about the connection between land, power and identity are timeless and universal and come through loud and clear.

Nothing's Changed crunched:

HARD – HEELS – GRASSES – SEEDS – CANS – CRUNCH – PURPLE-FLOWERING – AMIABLE – SIX – NO – KNOW – HANDS – SKIN – LUNGS – HOT – ANGER – BRASH – FLAG – SQUATS – WEEDS – HAUTE – GUARD – ONLY – SIGN – BELONG – PRESS – KNOW – WILL – WHITE – LINEN – ROSE – ROAD – WORKING – CHOWS – EAT – PLASTIC – WIPE – SPIT – BONE – BACK – BOY – MEAN – MOUTH – BURN – BOMB – SHIVER – NOTHING'S.

BATHING SCENE, FAIRFIELD BEACH, FAIRFIELD, CONN.

Sophie Hannah, *Postcard from a Travel Snob*

For the stage

Poems such as *Nothing's Changed* and *London* demand to be read out loud, preferably fiercely, preferably from a stage, preferably to a politically-charged audience. Afrika's and Blake's poems have a clear purpose – to hit home hard and to persuade their readers and even to spark a response. With its comic punchline - 'an anthropologist in shorts' - we might imagine Hannah's poem also to be recited from a stage, but in this case a comedy stage would be more fitting. This poet's gentler intention is to amuse us with her satirical, ironic wit.

As the inversion of the common holiday postcard cliché, 'wish you were here!' in the first line immediately establishes, the superior speaker of this breezy dramatic monologue rejects conventional, package-type holidays and eschews the tired, chintzy language often used on postcards home to describe them. He or she is not staying at anywhere as common as a 'holiday resort' or as tacky as a 'seaside-town'; they will not be found caterwauling boozily during 'karaoke nights' or propped up at the bar knocking back 'pints of beer', or even glugging 'sangria' in the sun. Oh, no, they are far, far too classy for any of that sort of vulgarity.

What the superior speaker wishes for on their holiday is isolation [especially from other typical English tourists], peace and virginal nature 'untouched by man'. They embrace authenticity and quirky originality, even accepting discomfort to achieve this: 'I'm sleeping in a local farmer's van'.

Perish the thought

All dramatic monologues feature ironic gaps between how the speaker thinks they are coming across and how their puppet masters, the poets, really want  them to appear. Imagine, for instance, how this speaker would expect us to respond to their words. Imagine them at a suitably middle class social event, perhaps a dinner party with a few good friends with similar views, boasting about their holiday adventures, swilling a glass of wine. The speaker would expect nods of agreement, knowing chuckles in the right places, wry smiles, interest and even admiration. When they use a phrase such as 'rest assured' they indicate that they expect their audience to share their views. And the poem is funny because through satire it skewers this pompous speaker's ridiculous pretensions and because it is likely to make many adult readers squirm in awkward recognition of something close to our own attitudes.

We may find that we're caught somewhere in between in our attitudes. After all, though they may be a snob looking down their nose at other people, it is understandable, isn't it, that the speaker wants a different type of holiday from the norm? We might, or might not, share their feelings about drunken karaoke and we're likely to recognise their description of over commercialised sea-side towns. But we're also laughing at this character as well as with them. There's something pernickety and fastidious about the phrase 'perish the thought', expressing the sense of the speaker that their's is the only right way to think. Different people choose different holidays and that's fine, of course. But this speaker expresses distaste for other people's choices and it's this snobbery that makes them comically unsympathetic. They are patronising and insulting about other holiday makers, meanly calling them 'small-minded-package-Philistine-abroad' types. Clearly 'sleeping' in a 'farmer's van' is a preposterously extreme way of avoiding conventional holiday accommodation. But it's in the final stanza that Hannah really lays on the irony and turns the humour most strongly against her opinionated speaker.

Almost every line is ridiculous and, worse, self-deceiving. A culture or a region can be multicultural, but it's not possible for a single person to be 'multi-cultural'. Having sneered at holiday makers who drink beer and sangria, the speaker refers to their friends approvingly as 'wine connoisseurs'. Presumably drunken 'wine connoisseurs' behave in a much more refined and cultured ways than common 'drunks'. The speaker might not be a British tourist 'in the sea', but they're still a British tourist, in a van. And, in fact, they are in the 'sea' just like everyone else, but in a final flourish of self-regard they call themselves an 'anthropologist'. Yeah, sure, whatever you say. Such preening self-aggrandisement and an inflated sense of self-importance is underlined by the fact that almost a third of the poem's lines start with the first-person pronoun 'I'.

The confident, bouncy regular pentameter [e.g. 'this **place** is **not** a **holiday** re**sort**'] works with a regular cross-rhyme scheme of full rhymes to generate the poem's breeziness. The pattern gives the poem a predictability so that, after the first few lines, the ear anticipates the rhyming pattern and the satisfying sonic completion this will achieve at the end of each stanza. Rhymes click neatly into place, adding to the sense that the speaker is expressing their views confidently, even complacently. And, mirroring the speaker's firmly fixed mindset, there is no change at all in either the rhyme pattern or the stanza form.

A striking linguistic feature of this dramatic monologue is the use of the two long, compounding phrases, in which multiple words are strung together:

- 'Seaside-town-consumer-hell'

- 'Sun-and-sangria-two-weeks-small-minded-package-philistine-abroad'.

Neatly, this lumping of words together reflects the speaker's sweeping generalizations about other people and places that are not to his or her taste. Like other speakers in this cluster of poems, this character reveals his or her own identity in relation to their attitude to places. Like other speakers, this character also defines their sense of self in oppositional terms, in this instance based on taste and class.

Postcard from a Travel Snob crushed:

I – RESORT – KARAOKE – DRUNKEN – UNTOUCHED – HELL – VAN – NOT – NOBODY – ASSURED – SANGRIA – PHILISTINE – MULT-CULTURAL – CONNOISSEURS – TOURIST – ANTHROPOLOGIST.

John Davidson, *In Romney Marsh*

Musical painting

A dynamic, noisy and vibrantly colourful poem, this celebration of a particular English landscape is delivered with great gusto. From the outset the poet signals the key foci of the poem - movement ['I went down'], sounds ['I heard'] and visuals ['I saw']. And, indeed, Davidson packs his orderly quatrains with visual, sonic and kinaesthetic imagery, repeats mood defining words, skilfully manages vowel and consonant sounds and sets the whole thing off on emphatically bouncy, predominantly regular lines of cross-rhymed tetrameters.

There are lots of references to colour in the poem and the poet employs an intensely rich palette, one that ranges from yellow to orange and from blue to purple to red: 'Yellow sunlight', 'saffron beach', 'sapphire' [sky], 'a veil of purple', 'roses', 'crimson bands'. In the penultimate stanza, Davidson adds 'silver fire', developing the pattern of comparing aspects of the landscape to precious things - 'saffron', 'sapphire', 'diamond', 'silver'. Combining with, and augmenting, the poem's visual intensity, the sonic imagery is just as rich. There are high notes, generated by the shrill 'ringing' of the 'wire from Romney', deeper, base notes, generated by the 'roar' of the waves and something in between, the sound of the beach that recalls bells 'pealing'. The importance of the words carrying these key sounds is underscored by their repetition - 'shrilly', 'shrill' x 2; 'ringing', 'rang'; 'pealed', 'pealing'.

Word music

Davidson's choice of words and their orchestration adds further layers to the poem's sonic texture. Take, for example, the second stanza. Assonance is put to work hard here, setting off the thin, high sound of the wires through the short 'i' of 'ringing shrilly' which is carried into the next line's 'within the wind' [where the alliteration of w's sets off a whistling effect] and ends, almost petering out, in the last line's 'its'. A longer 'i' sound is introduced by 'lithe' and runs through 'wire' to finish in 'Hythe'. The long vowel sound of 'taut' is carried through 'core',

and is part of a general pattern of sounds opening up and becoming rounder as the stanza progresses: 'O' vowels, both short, as in 'Romney' and 'along', and the longer 'ows' of 'sound', 'town', and 'wound' - take over from and eventually dominate the shorter 'i's. Syntax, metre and rhyme scheme add to the sonic effect. The final 'i' sound in the last line, for instance, falls only on an unstressed function word, 'its', whereas the o's of 'along' and 'wound' are stressed, with the latter taking further emphasis through being both the stanza's final word and its final rhyme.

Or take a few other examples from across the poem. At times Davidson stitches watery sibilance - streams of 's' sounds - with punchy plosives and rolling r's into the sonic texture of the poem. Stanza four is especially marked by these patterns and culminates with plosives, such as 'diamond drops', 'beach/ beads', 's' sounds - running through 'saffron', 'drops', beads', 'surge' - a gradually building, rolling 'r' pattern, from 'saffron' - 'drop' - 'surge' - 'pro' - 'roar' as well as an opening up and widening of the vowels as the stanza develops. A similar method is used in the final stanza. Here a rich variety of 's' sounds culminates in 'stops', a long 'ee' whistles through 'sea' to 'stream' to 'beach' and 'peal', and 'organ' picks up the key sounds from 'shore' and sends them resonating onwards to be completed in 'roar'. The metaphor of 'organ stops' also, of course, emphasises the musical way in which the poet perceives and presents this landscape.

Adding to the poem's glowing and sonic vibrancy are the words stressing movement: The flowers 'flow', the wire winds, the masts 'wagged', the waves are 'swinging', beads of surf 'surge', sunlight flickers, night 'sank', salt sea drops, 'streamed', the waves 'clashed'. From morning to night, from light to darkness, the whole vivid landscape it seems is nosily jostling together in restless motion.

Captivated and captured

Though he was a Victorian writer, Davidson's poem could be classified as a Late Romantic lyric. It features a first-person narrator who travels alone into nature and finds inspiration within it. Compare this poem to ones by probably the most famous of landscape poets, William Wordsworth, and Davidson's lack of ego becomes more obvious. The poet is there in the poem, present, but very much keeping to the background. He gives to himself the most colourless of words and the simplest syntax - 'I went', 'I heard', 'I saw'. The star of the show in this poem is most definitely the wild landscape itself, not its effect on the poet's character, psyche or development. All Davidson's artistic energies have gone into trying to find language that is as vibrant and vivid and dynamic as the thing it tries to capture.

'Capture' is an important verb in this context. Because as well as trying to replicate linguistically the sounds, sights and movements he witnessed, Davidson also shows mastery of these materials in his arrangement of the poem. Though, as we have seen and heard, each stanza is packed with dynamic energies, these are channelled and controlled by the forces of syntax, metre and form. Each of the stanzas is, for instance, composed of a single sentence that flows from the first line to the last and each sentence and stanza ends in a full stop at the end of the final line. The waves may roar and crash, the wires whistle, and stars come down in a 'great shower', but this is all contained in neat, repeated orderliness. Similarly, though there are a few trochaic substitutions here and there, the poem runs along a smoothe and emphatic tetrameter and maintains its cross-rhymed scheme with full, masculine rhymes throughout. This is a robust, solidly-built poem with regular metre, stanzas and rhyme. Such as a form could be read as ironically being in contrast with the wild energies of wind and waves, or as expressing the poet's capacity to be captivated by, but also to control and capture this subject.

In Romney Marsh crunched:

I - SING - SAW - NORMAN - RINGING - WIND - WIRE - WOUND - PURPLE - FRINGE - SAPPHIRE - HEAVEN'S - WAGGED - SWINGING - DIAMOND - SURGE - DYMCHURCH - DOWNS - CRIMSON - FLICKER - SILVER - STARS - SHRILL - RANG - SHINING - CLASHED - BEACH - ROAR

Elizabeth Jennings, *Absence*

Imagine that a student or a friend writes a description of a painful loss they have experienced recently and then asks you to read their work and respond to it. Why might this be a tricky situation? What would you worry about? How would you set about judging their writing? Would it be on the strength of feelings they express or the technical accomplishment with which they express these? What if the sentiments were powerful, but the spelling and punctuation and grammar were dreadful? Would you be able to be honest in your response or would the danger of seeming insensitive weigh heavily on your mind? Tony Harrison crystallised the sort of critical dilemma you might face when he wrote about the words chosen for his mother's gravestone. As a poet, Harrison was expected to produce something eloquent, but found that he couldn't express the feelings better than his uneducated father. Even though his father's writing was 'misspelt, mawkish, stylistically appalling', the poet admits he couldn't 'squeeze more love' into the words.[6]

There are many difficulties about writing about loss. The material is obviously

---

[6] From *Book Ends II*.

highly personal and sensitive, the emotions potentially so strong it might be hard to find some artistic distance. On the one hand, producing the poem might be a form of therapy for writers - writing about a topic helping them to process the experience of grief. But, on the other hand, there may be guilt at turning such personal experience into art in the first place, as well as fear that the poem will not be up to the task, fear even that the poem will do the loss an injustice.

Still waters running deep

Although she didn't follow The Movement poets' ironic stance or share their atheism, Jennings does share with writers such as Philip Larkin and Kingsley Amis a conversational, unshowy and understated style that was a key part of the Movement aesthetic. In addition, Jennings' traditional English poetic virtues - traditional English forms, neat, regular stanzas, clear rhyme schemes with rhymes cropping up where we'd expect them at the ends of lines, general intelligibility and rationality – are also qualities associated with the work of Larkin and co. But perhaps only a modest and religiously-inclined poet would expect and welcome some external force to 'instruct' her on how to behave when dealing with emotions as powerful as grief.

There's an evenness of tone, a steadiness and neatness of composition and a gentleness to *Absence* that reflects the well-tended gardens the poet is visiting. Underneath the poem's quiet, well-mannered, very English surface, there is, of course, terrible pain and overwhelming grief, but these unsettling feelings are just about kept under control. In similar circumstances an American confessional poet writing at about the same time as Jennings would probably have let rip and produced a great, raging howl of a poem. However, Jennings is very English, very understated and deals with difficult, unruly emotions with a steady hand. On the surface, this self-control might even suggest, to an inattentive reader, that she is rather cold and untroubled, even unfeeling. It would be a mistake, however, to think raw emotions are not there; they are, but they are kept tucked away under the poem's surface, implied rather than stated. Like Thomas Hardys' in *Where the Picnic Was*, Jennings' method requires the reader to pick up and fill in some of this emotional subtext. Whether the understated approach makes the poem less or more powerful than our imaginary American howl of anguish is up to you to decide.

The key attributes of the place the poet, or her first-person narrator, visits are its orderliness and constancy: The gardens are 'well-tended', the jet from the fountains is 'steady'. Even the breeze is 'level'. The fountain's jet is also 'usual', there is 'no sign that anything had ended' and, indeed, 'nothing' has 'changed', a fact emphasised by being repeated, 'the place was just the same'. The world seems big, solid, civilised, dependable and we might assume that this would be a source of comfort to the speaker. But, in the second stanza we learn that she feels disconnected from the world around her; she is unable to share the 'ecstasy' of the birds' singing. And, in fact, the orderliness and constancy and dependability of the world is not comforting, it makes the addressee's absence hit home harder as a 'savage force'. The adjective here gains added impact from being so incongruous with all the civilised rationality of both the place and the poem's matching diction that has preceded it. On the surface, things seem calm in this poem, but 'under all the gentleness' the speaker senses 'an earthquake tremor', the ground shifting to destabilise everything, a 'tremor' triggered only by recalling for a moment the absent beloved's name. The force of this absence is so strong that it changes everything.

You may have noticed that I've shifted a little myself in this essay. Having begun by assuming that the poem's narrator is the poet herself, I've then qualified this assumption and used the more neutral term 'speaker', which could refer to a

character the poet has made up. This is because Jennings insisted that she did not write autobiographical poetry and also because we should never assume that a poem necessarily expresses direct, lived experience in the perspective of the poet. Nevertheless, the distinction makes little difference in this particular case, no earthquake tremor that would shake our reading of the poem into new perspectives.

The level breeze and the savage force

As we have seen, Jennings' poem is characterised by the steadiness and good orderliness of its composition, evinced in its diction and tone as well as by its formal features. The poem's stanza are robust blocks of text, laid out in longish lines and end neatly in their final lines with emphatic full stops. The metre is iambic pentameter and operates with clockwork regularity. Scan the lines and you'll find that occasionally Jennings uses a trochee at the start instead of an iamb, but the vast majority of lines fall into controlled, steady iambs, even the lines that introduce the rawest emotions:

'That **made** your **ab**sence **seem** a **sav**age **force**.'

The end-rhymes also fall into place with well-tended precision. All these features match and accentuate the rational, reflective speaker, examining her own responses with dutiful care. Together they form the poem's 'level breeze', its steady, even breathing.

But read the poem more closely and you'll detect a subtle counter force operating under the poem's carefully balanced surface. For example, at times the metrical stress pattern conflicts with the rhyme pattern. In the eighth line, for example, if the caesura is read as an unstressed beat, to maintain the iambic structure the last three words should be stressed '**sure**ly **in** these'. But because 'these' rhymes with the preceding 'trees' it inevitably takes sonic emphasis, an effect only slightly quieted by the use of enjambment. A tiny ripple in the fabric, or discord in the poem's melody, admittedly. But here's another: quatrains are balanced because they have four lines with two rhymes. Jennings uses cinquains, which means there must be an uneven balance of rhymes, 3/2 in each stanza. Moreover, in the last stanza the most unbalancing thing in the whole poem, the 'savage force' is not rhymed back into good order – its echoing line ends with 'birds and grass'. Overall the more powerful force may be the level breeze, but every now and again, this breeze is disturbed and troubled.

Another subtle way in which Jennings makes the poem poignant is by writing it to the presumably dead beloved, as if she is speaking quietly to them. As the first line establishes where once there was a 'we' now that is only a solitary 'I'. Moreover, Jennings places the reader in the role of the addressee, but holds the full force of this back until the last stanza. Hence the phrase 'your absence' comes a little as a shock, and having been delayed, has a greater impact.

Absence crunched:

WE – WELL-TENDED – STEADY – ENDED – FORGET – THOUGHTLESS – ECSTASY – SURELY – PAIN – DISCORD – BECAUSE – SAVAGE – UNDER – EARTHQUAKE – NAME.

Comparing the poems

In the exam you will have to complete two poetry tasks, both comparative in nature. In the first you'll be asked to compare a specific poem printed on the paper with any one from the anthology of your choice. In the second task you're required to compare two unseen poems. For the first question you have 35 minutes, for the second you've 45 minutes. No doubt it will have struck you that 35 minutes is not a lot of time to write a decent comparative essay. What you certainly cannot afford to do is dilly dally over the choice of the second poem. If you've prepared thoroughly for this exam you will have already matched up all the poems in several different possible combinations, so that as soon as you see the printed poem you'll already know to which poem you're going to compare it. Not only that, but you should also have worked out the key points of comparison and contrast.

According to Edexcel, 'responses that are considerably unbalanced' will not reach the top grades, so you can't write predominantly on one of the poems. The examiners are also looking for 'perceptive comparison' on a range of 'similarities and differences'. Significantly, for a top grade as well as evaluating the poets' use of language, showing an excellent understanding of context and employing precise terminology, you have to develop a 'perceptive grasp of form and structure'. Often this is the most challenging aspect of poetry for pupils and, hence, it's an aspect we've covered in detail in each of our essays.

The best way to develop an overview of the relationships between these poems is to write down all the titles on a large piece of paper. First, map out what the poems have in common and after how they are different to each other. It's very useful to have one piece of paper that captures these textual relationships. Use colour, arrows, icons, venn diagrams, anything that helps make the connections memorable. Another useful exercise that can be done time and again in the run up to the exam is to write the titles of all the poems on paper, cut these out individually, turn them over and then pick up three pieces of paper randomly. The task then is to say how two of the poems are similar and how the third is different. Do this quickly, a couple of minutes or so, in order that you focus on key aspects. Put the titles back in the mix, pick three more at random and repeat the exercise, over and over again.

Self-evidently there are many different ways in which these poems could be grouped to aid comparison. They could, for instance, be arranged in terms of poems that are most unlike, as this would help us to focus on the differences rather than the similarities between a disparate collection of poems. Which poems are least alike? Perhaps, superficially at least, the ones most separated furthest by time - the oldest poem in the cluster, Blake's *London* seems to have little in common with one of the most modern poems, Hannah's *Postcard from a Travel Snob*. Tonally the poems couldn't be more dissimilar - Blake's fierce poem is an excoriating indictment of corruption in society, whereas Hannah's is a lightly comic, wry piece of social satire. But even in this case, there are overlaps. Both poems are, for instance, written in regular quatrains, both use emphatic end-rhymes, to some extent both are written in a demotic style, both are written in the lyric voice, and so forth. Nevertheless, there are a far more differences than similarities between these two poems, and, as we suggested in our introductory section, the most successful comparative essays use poems that have a good balance of things that link them and that make them distinctive from each other.

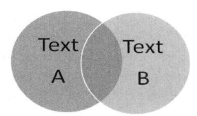

As with the essays that precede this section, what follows is not intended to be an exhaustive or comprehensive list of the ways in which the poems can be grouped or compared to be followed uncritically. Rather these groups are designed to prompt further thinking and development. So, one obvious way to arrange the poems is by chronology. Broadly, the poems fall into four chronological groups:

Romantic poems	Victorian	Early C20th	Mid - late C20th
London Composed Upon Westminster Bridge To Autumn	I Started Early Home Thoughts from Abroad	Where the Picnic was Adlestrop In Romney Marsh	Absence Stewart Island First Flight Nothing's Changed Hurricane Hits England Postcard from a Travel Snob Presents from my Aunts in Pakistan

What do the oldest poems have in common? Firstly, we now call this loose band of poets The Romantics and label their work as examples of Romantics. Blake and Wordsworth were part of the first wave and Keats part of the second wave of the Romantic movement, a radical change that swept through all the arts in the late eighteenth century. This is not to say, however, that these poems are necessarily more alike than they are different. Though they all feature nature, for instance, it is configured in very different ways. Blake's poem could, for instance, be read as an anti-pastoral, the corrupting city the antithesis of nurturing natural landscapes. Though he uses nature as the ultimate index of beauty, Wordsworth's poem is also urban in setting. Although both express strong emotions in typically Romantic fashion, the emotions in these two poems are almost opposite. Like Wordsworth, Keats is celebrating natural beauty, in his case the beauty of an underappreciated season. Where Wordsworth's diction is heightened and soulful, Blake's stark and symbolic, Keats' is noticeably more sensual. Though they make different choices, each of these Romantic poets writes within a recognisable and traditional poetic form – Wordsworth chooses the sonnet, Blake writes a lyric and Keats needs the more commodious form of the Ode.

Is there a distinctive style to the group of early twentieth century poems? One of them must have been written earlier, so that seems unlikely. Davidson died in 1909, so, unless he wrote the poem posthumously, it must have been published over a decade after it was written. Nevertheless, Davidson's poem shares Georgian poetry's gentle celebrations of gentle countryside, though the poetic mode sounds more heightened, less conversational and less modern than Edward Thomas adopts in *Adlestrop*. Though working in more traditional form than Thomas, Thomas Hardy also employs a more down-to-earth diction than Davidson. Its themes are personal loss also gives Hardy's poem a greater societal resonance due to being composed on the cusp of WWI. As a lament, in some ways, however, Hardy's poem has most in common with Jennings' poem about personal loss, *Absence*. This is unsurprisingly as the Movement poets saw Hardy as a guiding light in terms of subject matter, understated tone and innovation within traditional poetic forms.

Another way of highlighting the links between the poems would be to break down time and place into subcategories, based on tone, setting, attitude and so forth. Considering the kind of exam question you will face, this seems a particularly useful grouping strategy. Some poems, will, of course, appear in several categories or groupings.

Grouping #1

Though it has a somewhat melancholic, wistful air, **Keats' ode** is a celebration of the season, a time of year, rather than a place. **Wordsworth's sonnet** is also celebratory, but with undercurrents of more complex tones. While Wordsworth is praising a place, London, and not a time of year, his exultant mood is also triggered by the time of day, the morning – the dawn being a traditional symbol of new hope and new beginnings. In this celebratory group we could also place Browning's nostalgic *Home Thoughts*, Thomas' wistful *Adlestrop* and Davidson's lyrical *In Romney Marsh*. All of these poems also celebrate distinctly English scenes – though Keats doesn't specify that he is describing an English autumn, the fauna, flora and 'mellow' weather makes this pretty clear. Though Wordsworth is rhapsodising about an urban landscape, the paragon of beauty he compares it to is a natural landscape of hills and valleys. Unlike Browning's and Davidson's poems, Thomas' shares with *To Autumn* a sense of a beautiful, heightened space of time that is the more beautiful for being transient.

Grouping #2

The sense of melancholy that arguably pervades Keats' and Thomas' poems could link them to other poems more obviously focused on loss, in particular Jennings' *Absence* and Hardy's *Where the Picnic Was*. In *Adlestrop* the poet hears the solitary bird song and this sonic thread connects the solitary speaker to all the birdsong surrounding him. In contrast Jennings' feels a disconnection with the 'ecstasy' of bird song. All four of these poems are also about inevitable change and a change for the worse. Keats' autumn, like Thomas's Adlestrop is a liminal space. **Keats' ode** is set in a half-way space, in the transition between summer and winter, with the latter carrying ominous associations connected to mortality [the image of bird flight at the end of the poem is a classic symbol of approaching death]. Thomas's poem features an arrested journey and a brief contemplative pause before the dramatic and tragic transition that awaits just beyond the poem's last words. Jennings' relationship with the well-tended gardens, like Hardy's with the familiar coastal path, is shaped by a time before and a time now that are irreconcilable because of a tragic loss. Stylistically the latter two poems also share a stoical and understated manner.

Grouping #3

Several other poems share a distinct 'before and after'/ 'then and now' aspect – *Nothing's Changed* springs to mind - or feature literal and/or metaphorical journeys. Like Alvi's, **Emily Dickinson's poem** has two locations and the speaker moves between the two. In the American poet's case, they are the town and the sea, and the poet/ speaker goes on a journey out and back again that seems seminal. *First Flight* and *Postcard from a Travel Snob* also include journeys to or between places. Up in the air, Fanthorpe's poem shares with Thomas's a liminal space, though in the former's case the dominant feeling is of detachment. In *Hurricane Hits England* the journey taken by the weather is mirrored by an internal journey of discovery experienced by the protagonist.

Grouping #4

Blake's *London* shares with **Wordsworth's sonnet** its description of an urban landscape and specifically the capital itself, of course. Tonally, however, as in their perspectives, the poems couldn't be much more different. Many of the poems in the cluster present positive images of places. Like Afrika's *Nothing's Changed* and Adcock's unsentimental *Stewart Island*, Blake's attitude is much more critical and damning. Afrika's and Blake's urban poems also share a sense of righteous anger at injustice.

Group #5

Several of the poems concern the relationship between place and a sense of self. In **Emily Dickinson poem**, the speaker's sense of self is conceived in oppositional and gendered terms. At first it seems that in *Presents from My Aunts in Pakistan*, Alvi is also exploring her divided sense of self through the oppositions between her English and Pakistani heritage. However, in Alvi's case the poem itself forms a more hopeful option – a hybrid self enriched and informed by both cultures. A similar development can be recognised in Nichols' poem, *Hurricane Hits England*. Initially the woman in the poem feels separated from and isolated in her host culture. It takes the stirring violence of the storm to shift her perceptions and form the universal links between all humanity. Though it is not the poem's main focus, Afrika's poem also explores identity. The speaker in *Nothing's Changed* also defines himself in binary terms, not by gender or nationality, but by class and race. Unlike the other poems in this grouping, Afrika's doesn't hold out the possibility of a happy unifying resolution to apparently intractable division. *Hannah's dramatic monologue* puts a comic and ironic spin on the identity issue, with another speaker who defines themselves in opposition, here based on taste as well as class. For this speaker, the places we like and visit reveal who we are just as much as where we come from and where we live.

There are, of course, a myriad of ways to group and compare these poems. We could, for instance, put the poems written by English writers and about England together. Or we could make a group of the poems written by female poets. Would there be anything distinctive about the latter? Perhaps, perhaps not.

A sonnet of revision activities

1. Reverse millionaire: 10,000 points if students can guess the poem just from one word from it. You can vary the difficulty as much as you like. For example, 'clams', would be fairly easily identifiable as from Sexton's poem whereas 'fleet' would be more difficult. 1000 points if students can name the poem from a single phrase or image – 'portion out the stars and dates'. 100 points for a single line. 10 points for recognising the poem from a stanza. Play individually or in teams.

2. Research the poet. Find one sentence about them that you think sheds light on their poem in the anthology. Compare with your classmates. Or find a couple more lines or a stanza by a poet and see if others can recognise the writer from their lines.

3. Write a cento based on one or more of the poems. A cento is a poem constructed from lines from other poems. Difficult, creative, but also fun, perhaps.

4. Read 3 or 4 other poems by one of the poets. Write a pastiche. See if classmates can recognise the poet you're imitating.

5. Write the introduction for a critical guide on the poems aimed at next year's yr. 10 class.

6. Use the poet Glynn Maxwell's typology of poems to arrange the poems into different groups. In his excellent book, *On Poetry*, Maxwell suggests poems have four dominant aspects, which he calls solar, lunar, musical and visual. A solar poem hits home, is immediately striking. A lunar poem, by contrast, is more mysterious and might not give up its meanings so easily. Ideally a lunar poem will haunt your imagination. Written mainly for the ear, a musical poem focuses on the sounds of language, rather than the meanings. Think of Lewis Carroll's

Jabberwocky. A visual poem is self-conscious about how it looks to the eye. Concrete poems are the ultimate visual poems. According to Maxwell, the very best poems are strong in each dimension. Try applying this test to each poem. Which ones come out on top?

7. Maxwell also recommends conceptualising the context in which the words of the poem are created or spoken. Which poems would suit being read around a camp fire? Which would be better declaimed from the top of a tall building? Which might you imagine on a stage? Which ones are more like conversation overheard? Which are the easiest and which the most difficult to place?

8. Mr Maxwell is a fund of interesting ideas. He suggests all poems dramatise a battle between the forces of whiteness and blackness, nothingness and somethingness, sound and silence, life and death. In each poem, what is the dynamic between whiteness and blackness? Which appears to have the upper hand?

9. Still thinking in terms of evaluation, consider the winnowing effect of time. Which of the modern poems do you think might be still read in 20, a 100 or 200 years? Why?

10. Give yourself only the first and last line of one of the poems. Without peeking at the original, try to fill in the middle. Easy level: write in prose. Expert level: attempt verse.

11. According to Russian Formalist critics, poetry performs a 'controlled explosion on ordinary language'. What evidence can you find in this selection of controlled linguistic detonations?

12. A famous musician once said that though he wasn't the best at playing all the notes, nobody played the silences better. In Japanese garden water features the sound of a water drop is designed to make us notice the silence around it. Try reading one of the poems in the light of these

comments, focusing on the use of white space, caesuras, punctuation – all the devices that create the silence on which the noise of the poem rests.

13. In *Notes on the Art of Poetry*, Dylan Thomas wrote that 'the best craftsmanship always leaves holes and gaps in the works of the poem so that something that is not in the poem can creep, crawl, flash or thunder in'. Examine a poem in the light of this comment, looking for its holes and gaps. If you discover these, what 'creeps', 'crawls' or 'flashes' in to fill them?

14. Different types of poems conceive the purpose of poetry differently. Broadly speaking Augustan poets of the eighteenth century aimed to impress their readers with the wit of their ideas and the elegance of the expression. In contrast, Romantic poets wished to move their readers' hearts. Characteristically Victorian poets aimed to teach the readers some kind of moral principle or example. Self-involved, avant-garde Modernists weren't overly bothered about finding, never mind pleasing, a general audience. What impact do the Edexcel anthology poems seek? Do they seek to amuse, appeal to the heart, teach us something? Are they like soliloquies – the overheard inner workings of thinking – or more like speeches or mini-plays? Try placing each poem somewhere on the following continuums. Then create a few continuums of your own. As ever, comparison with your classmates will prove illuminating.

Emotional..intellectual

Feelings...ideas

Internal..external

Contemplative...rhetorical

Open..guarded

Terminology task

The following is a list of poetry terminology and short definitions of the terms. Unfortunately, cruel, malicious individuals (i.e. us) have scrambled them up. Your task is to unscramble the list, matching each term to the correct definition. Good luck!

Term	Definition
Imagery	Vowel rhyme, e.g. 'bat' and 'lag'
Metre	An implicit comparison in which one thing is said to be another
Rhythm	
Simile	Description in poetry
Metaphor	A conventional metaphor, such as a 'dove' for peace
Symbol	A metrical foot comprising an unstressed followed by a stressed beat
Iambic	
Pentameter	A line with five beats
Enjambment	Description in poetry using metaphor, simile or personification
Caesura	
Dramatic monologue	A repeated pattern of ordered sound
Figurative imagery	An explicit comparison of two things, using 'like' or 'as'
Onomatopoeia	Words, or combinations of words, whose sounds mimic their meaning
Lyric	
Adjective	Words in a line starting with the same letter or sound
Alliteration	A strong break in a line, usually signalled by punctuation
Ballad	A regular pattern of beats in each line
Sonnet	A narrative poem with an alternating four and three beat line
Assonance	
Sensory imagery	A word that describes a noun
Quatrain	A 14-line poem following several possible rhyme schemes
Diction	When a sentence steps over the end of a line and continues into the next line or stanza
Personification	
	Description that uses the senses
	A four-line stanza
	Inanimate objects given human characteristics
	A poem written in the voice of a character
	A poem written in the first person, focusing on the emotional experience of the narrator
	A term to describe the vocabulary used in a poem.

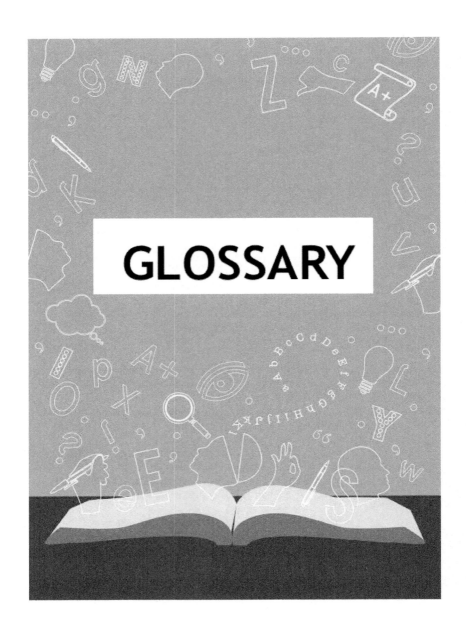

GLOSSARY

ALLITERATION – the repetition of consonants at the start of neighbouring words in a line

ANAPAEST - a three beat pattern of syllables, unstress, unstress, stress. E.g. 'on the moon', 'to the coast', 'anapaest'

ANTITHESIS - the use of balanced opposites

APOSTROPHE – a figure of speech addressing a person, object or idea

ASSONANCE – vowel rhyme, e.g. sod and block

BLANK VERSE – unrhymed lines of iambic pentameter

BLAZON – a male lover describing the parts of his beloved

CADENCE – the rise of fall of sounds in a line of poetry

CAESURA – a distinct break in a poetic line, usually marked by punctuation

COMPLAINT – a type of love poem concerned with loss and mourning

CONCEIT – an extended metaphor

CONSONANCE – rhyme based on consonants only, e.g. book and back

COUPLET – a two-line stanza, conventionally rhyming

DACTYL – the reverse pattern to the anapaest; stress, unstress, unstress. E.g. 'Strong as a'

DRAMATIC MONOLOGUE – a poem written in the voice of a distinct character

ELEGY – a poem in mourning for someone dead

END-RHYME – rhyming words at the end of a line

END-STOPPED – the opposite of enjambment; i.e. when the sentence and the poetic line stop at the same point

ENJAMBMENT – where sentences run over the end of lines and stanzas

FIGURATIVE LANGUAGE – language that is not literal, but employs figures of speech, such as metaphor, simile and personification

FEMININE RHYME – a rhyme that ends with an unstressed syllable or unstressed syllables.

FREE VERSE – poetry without metre or a regular, set form

GOTHIC – a style of literature characterised by psychological horror, dark deeds and uncanny events

HEROIC COUPLETS – pairs of rhymed lines in iambic pentameter

HYPERBOLE – extreme exaggeration

IAMBIC – a metrical pattern of a weak followed by a strong stress, ti-TUM, like a heart beat

IMAGERY – the umbrella term for description in poetry. Sensory imagery refers to descriptions that appeal to sight, sound and so forth; figurative imagery refers to the use of devices such as metaphor, simile and personification

JUXTAPOSITION – two things placed together to create a strong contrast

LYRIC – an emotional, personal poem usually with a first-person speaker

MASCULINE RHYME – an end rhyme on a strong syllable

METAPHOR – an implicit comparison in which one thing is said to be another

METAPHYSICAL – a type of poetry characterised by wit and extended metaphors

METRE – the regular pattern organising sound and rhythm in a poem

MOTIF – a repeated image or pattern of language, often carrying thematic significance

OCTET OR OCTAVE – the opening eight lines of a sonnet

ONOMATOPOEIA – bang, crash, wallop

PENTAMETER – a poetic line consisting of five beats

PERSONIFICATION – giving human characteristics to inanimate things

PLOSIVE – a type of alliteration using 'p' and 'b' sounds

QUATRAIN – a four-line stanza

REFRAIN – a line or lines repeated like a chorus

ROMANTIC – A type of poetry characterised by a love of nature, by strong emotion and heightened tone

SESTET – the last six lines in a sonnet

SIMILE – an explicit comparison of two different things

SONNET – a form of poetry with fourteen lines and a variety of possible set rhyme patterns

SPONDEE – two strong stresses together in a line of poetry

STANZA – the technical name for a verse

SYMBOL – something that stands in for something else. Often a concrete representation of an idea.

SYNTAX – the word order in a sentence. doesn't Without sense English syntax make. Syntax is crucial to sense: For example, though it uses all the same words, 'the man eats the fish' is not the same as 'the fish eats the man'

TERCET – a three-line stanza

TETRAMETER – a line of poetry consisting of four beats

TROCHEE – the opposite of an iamb; stress, unstress, strong, weak.

VILLANELLE – a complex interlocking verse form in which lines are recycled

VOLTA – the 'turn' in a sonnet from the octave to the sestet

Recommended reading

Atherton, C., Green, A. & Snapper, G. Teaching English Literature 16-19. NATE, 2013

Bowen et al. The Art of Poetry, vol.1-18. Peripeteia Press, 2015-18

Brinton, I. Contemporary Poetry. CUP, 2009

Eagleton, T. How to Read a Poem. Wiley & Sons, 2006

Fry, S. The Ode Less Travelled. Arrow, 2007

Hamilton, I. & Noel-Todd, J. Oxford Companion to Modern Poetry, OUP, 2014

Herbert, W. & Hollis, M. Strong Words. Bloodaxe, 2000

Hurley, M. & O'Neill, M. Poetic Form, An Introduction. CUP, 2012

Meally, M. & Bowen, N. The Art of Writing English Literature Essays, Peripeteia Press, 2014

Maxwell, G. On Poetry. Oberon Masters, 2012

Padel, R. 52 Ways of Looking at a Poem. Vintage, 2004

Padel, R. The Poem and the Journey. Vintage, 2008

Paulin, T. The Secret Life of Poems. Faber & Faber, 2011

Schmidt, M. Lives of the Poets, Orion, 1998

Wolosky, S. The Art of Poetry: How to Read a Poem. OUP, 2008.

About the author

Head of English and freelance writer, Neil Bowen has a Masters Degree in Literature & Education from Cambridge University and is a member of Ofqual's experts panel for English. He is the author of *The Art of Writing English Essays for GCSE*, co-author of *The Art of Writing English Essays for A-level and Beyond* and of *The Art of Poetry*, volumes 1-18. Neil runs the peripeteia project, bridging the gap between A-level and degree level English courses: www.peripeteia.webs.com.